Helena

Helena Lee is the features director [...] for the magazine's art and culture [...] annual magazine *Bazaar Art*, celeb[...] women in the art world, and launched Bazaar Art Week in 2018, which was shortlisted for the BSME Best Innovation Award. In February 2020, she founded the platform East Side Voices to raise the visibility of talent of East and Southeast Asian heritage. She is a Platform Presents Playwright judge, a founding member of the Ginsburg Health Board, and a visiting lecturer at City University.

~

'Stunning and heartfelt . . . a must-read collection'
Kevin Kwan

'A strong, compelling, and quietly beautiful collection of stories that have gone untold for too long.'
Jonathan Liew

'The strength of this slim collection is in its nuance . . .
a thoughtful, painful reminder of the grand narratives that get buried under belittling stereotypes, of how progress can also regress and how self-actualisation, self-discovery and personal excellence still grate against the perceptions of strangers.'
Bidisha, *Observer*

'This important book, which is full of wit and insight, sheds light on aspects of racism that are often overlooked and it offers welcome exposure for a collection of voices that are too often sidelined from the cultural mainstream.'
Independent

'Wide-ranging in form and scope but always affecting'
New Statesman

Acknowledgements

Thank you…

…to all the incredible *East Side Voices* contributors: without your generosity, without your stories, this book would not exist. Your individual voices shine on their own, but together, they are devastatingly powerful. Special thanks to Tash Aw – you've been more instrumental to this whole project than you know, and also to Rowan Hisayo Buchanan, Sharlene Teo and Zing Tsjeng.

…to Francine Toon for your commitment, your vision, your brilliant insights, your partnership and patience. Thank you for the care you have taken over every single story. There were some difficult moments (nothing like a pandemic and four months of lockdown with children to disrupt a project!), which we've weathered together, and I am so honoured to have you as my editor. Thank you for making *East Side Voices* what it is.

…to the Sceptre team for your belief in *East Side Voices*, and especially Maria Garbutt-Lucero, herself an inspiration and brilliant ESEA advocate, and constant champion of *ESV*; Charlotte Humphery – for your judgment – you have been a much-needed stalwart this year; and Helen Flood – for whom no task is too big.

...to every single person who came to those first events; a big shout out to Rejina Pyo, Daisy Hoppen, Frances Cottrell-Duffield, Ben Spicer and the Standard Hotel, who gave East Side Voices the best start in life. Thanks also to Elaine Chong, who introduced me to the papers of Dr Diana Yeh and Dr Simone Knox.

... to my wonderful agents Sarah Chalfant and Jessica Bullock for your calm and incisive wisdom and invaluable counsel. And to Alba Ziegler-Bailey for helping to realise the change right from the start.

... to Viv Hsu, Anne Fuell, Sonia Tsukagoshi, Jo Ham, Claire Brayford, Iain Axon for the late-night calls, early reads, fact checks, design advice and years of love, and Mika Simmons, Gala Gordon, Bella Macpherson, Dee Acharya, Olive Wakefield, Melissa Hemsley, Edeline Lee, Erica Wagner for your friendship and all the incredible support. And, of course, my *Harper's Bazaar* family, especially Justine Picardie, Lydia Slater and Ella Alexander for championing this story in particular.

...to Mum and Dad, whose own journeys are ones to wonder at, and to learn from. Thank you for unquestioningly giving me everything you could, I am forever grateful.

The idea for the platform and the book began life, as all

good things seem to, at the kitchen table. Thank you, Tom for being my dinner-time consultant, video-editor, strategist, proof-reader, idea generator, sounding-board, extraordinary husband and even-better father all rolled into one. And thank you to my D&M. I'm so very proud of you. Everything I write is for you.

Join a literary community of
like-minded readers who seek out
the best in contemporary writing.

From the thousands of submissions Sceptre
receives each year, our editors select the books
we consider to be outstanding.

We look for distinctive voices, thought-provoking
themes, original ideas, absorbing narratives and
writing of prize-winning quality.

If you want to be the first to hear about our
new discoveries, and would like the chance to
receive advance reading copies of our books
before they are published, visit

www.sceptrebooks.co.uk

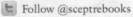 Follow @sceptrebooks

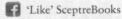 'Like' SceptreBooks

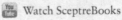 Watch SceptreBooks

Contents

EAST SIDE VOICES

*Essays celebrating East and Southeast Asian
identity in Britain*

Edited by Helena Lee

sceptre

First published in Great Britain in 2022 by Sceptre
An Imprint of Hodder & Stoughton
An Hachette UK company

This paperback edition published in 2022

2

A CIP catalogue record for this title is available from the British
Library

Paperback ISBN 9781529344509
eBook ISBN 9781529344486

Typeset in Sabon MT by
Palimpsest Book Production Ltd, Falkirk, Stirlingshire

Printed and bound in Great Britain by Clays Ltd, Elcograf S.p.A.

Hodder & Stoughton policy is to use papers that are natural,
renewable and recyclable products and made from wood grown in
sustainable forests. The logging and manufacturing processes are
expected to conform to the environmental regulations of the
country of origin.

Hodder & Stoughton Ltd
Carmelite House
50 Victoria Embankment
London EC4Y 0DZ

www.sceptrebooks.co.uk

Introduction

Helena Lee

I was rudely shaken out of my second maternity leave by Quentin Tarantino. It was the summer of 2019, and we were having a rare night out, watching the much-lauded film *Once Upon a Time in Hollywood*. Halfway through, we were confronted with the Cliff Booth versus Bruce Lee showdown in which Brad Pitt gets in a tussle with Mike Moh, who stars as the legendary martial artist but depicts him spouting philosophical nonsense, using dodgy noises and outdated kung fu tropes. Bruce Lee's ultimate humiliation – as a fighter at the top of his game unable to conquer this middle-aged white guy (who is, to be fair, played by Brad Pitt, so needs no validation) – sent the cinema around me wild. For them, this was by far the funniest part of the movie.

I was astounded. This was racial stereotyping; a racism that was completely unacknowledged by anyone around me. And yet I felt powerless to counter it. The whole film was intended as a reverential ode to the Hollywood greats, yet as part of that, Bruce Lee, the only non-white historical figure, was taken down. We hardly ever see an East or Southeast Asian face on screen, and when we do, they are there to serve as an object of mockery.

I began thinking about other depictions of Asians. There was the strange girl in the film *Pitch Perfect*, who mumbles inarticulately and is clearly constructed to be laughed at. I struggled to remember characters of East or Southeast Asian heritage in domestic dramas. And then there was the time when the footballer Diego Maradona was caught on camera accepting praise from a group of South Korean fans, but after he turned his back, pulled the sides of his eyes with his hands. The *Match of the Day* pundits shrugged a little uncomfortably, and the world's media laughed it off.

It was as though I wasn't within my rights to be outraged by any of this, because if I was, it wouldn't be acknowledged. Traditional campaigning media didn't seem to pick up the causes for East and Southeast Asians in Britain. People with faces like mine weren't being cast in lead roles for films or television series. If we were cast at all, then it would be for parts that required a Chinese accent, or was linked to a crime syndicate or was a typical Asian computer nerd – we seemed only qualified to act in the role of a racialised 'other'. The three-dimensional characters that reflected my own experience of growing up in the suburbs, of everyday family life, were scarce indeed.

Dr Diana Yeh articulated it well in her 2018 paper, in which she wrote: '"British Chinese" [a term ascribed to those perceived to fall into the category "Chinese"] cultural practices can, to cite Salman Rushdie (1988), be "visible but unseen", present in the social and cultural fabric but rendered invisible within the social and cultural imagination.'[1] Why weren't we considered for kitchen-sink dramas, helming documentaries, helping set the news agenda? If we weren't being represented in any meaningful way in mainstream media, that meant there was still an otherness to seeing an Asian face on screen. It was as though British East and Southeast Asians were an anonymous part of British culture. To me, it explained this empathy gap. Our stories weren't seen as valid enough to be told or reported on, and so we've long been excluded from the cultural canon. I certainly didn't want my children growing up in a world that did not see, acknowledge or validate them.

And so, in February 2020, East Side Voices was born. I wanted it to be a platform that aimed to change this outdated cultural narrative and combat these damaging stereotypes by amplifying the voices of those with East and Southeast Asian heritage who are living and shaping society here in Britain. And though the platform is open to everyone, I hoped to reach people who could help change the status quo – casting agents, literary agents, writers, journalists, directors; the people who frame the way we look at the

1 Diana Yeh, *The Cultural Politics of In/Visibility: Contesting 'British Chineseness' in the Arts*, in D. Yeh and A. Thorpe (Eds.), *Contesting British Chinese Culture*, Basingstoke, Hampshire: Palgrave Macmillan, 2018, pp. 31–59.

world through media. We were to meet once a month at a cultural salon, hearing from diasporic Asians with tales to tell. I thought it was important to glimpse into the experience of the diaspora as they are the link between all our cultures – occupying this rare space where they understand what it is to be British, but are also a bridge to ways of life we may be less familiar with. They help equip people with the vocabulary to talk about the complexities, richness and diversity of Asian identity in Britain. For that, we need good storytellers; stories are what help connect us.

East Side Voices launched with two events at the Standard Hotel in London, the first with the acclaimed novelists Sharlene Teo and Rowan Hisayo Buchanan, and the second with the fashion designer Rejina Pyo, each attended by everyone from national newspaper and magazine editors, film producers, publicists and photographers, to doctors and musicians, who listened, engaged, and talked with one another. When the opportunity to create this book appeared, it was the natural next step, and I couldn't wait to collect these powerful insights from talented writers from around the country into one place.

But then, the global pandemic swept in and destabilised the world. China, in particular, was spoken about with a lexicon of fear and derogatory tones. The then-US president Donald Trump referred to the 'China virus' and 'kung flu', aggravating the prejudice against the East and Southeast Asian diaspora that had always been there. In the UK, those of Black, Asian and minority ethnic backgrounds were disproportionately affected; to take one example, Filipinos make up the largest ethnic group of nurses in the NHS, and in May 2020, they were the single largest nationality to die from Covid-19. Police estimates suggest there was a threefold increase in racially-motivated hate crimes in London towards those of East and Southeast Asian heritage in the spring of 2020 compared with the same period the year before. The following October, when Parliament held its first-ever debate on racism experienced by the ESEA community, not one Conservative MP or government minister was present.

The pandemic also revealed that the media hardly considered these injustices important, and at times even contributed to the prejudice. Thirty-three per cent of images used by media outlets in the UK to report on Covid-19 featured Asian people, propounding the idea that the virus was specifically an Asian problem despite afflicting the whole world.

In March 2021, there was a mass shooting in which eight people were murdered at three spa and massage parlours in Atlanta. Six of the victims were Asian women, showing the devastating and tangible effects to cultural non-representation and racialised objectification. All the Asians I knew were deeply affected by this, but there wasn't much in the news that gave credence to our pain. It was against this backdrop that *The Sunday Times* ran a front-page story paying tribute to Prince Philip that referred to him as 'an often crochety figure, offending people with gaffes about slitty eyes, even if secretly we rather enjoyed them', thus not just offending the East and Southeast Asian communities at a time when they were considerably shaken, but also their own readers by suggesting they were racist. Who'd have thought we'd be so unprogressive and ignorant in the twenty-first century?

The mission of the book has therefore evolved from inspiring empathy and raising our voices through the magic of stories, to also breaking the cycle of systemic non-representation. There has been a groundswell of positive movement in the past few months. Even now, as I write, East Side Voices is starting work with the Commission for Diversity in the Public Realm with the Mayor of London. The #StopESEAHate campaign, spearheaded by the actress Gemma Chan (who also contributes to this collection), has launched, creating a centre of gravity for individuals, communities, allies, grassroots movements and pressure groups such as Besea.n and End the Virus of Racism, that are already doing such good work. And then there is talent like Emma Raducanu proudly making her heritage a big part of her story and becoming a worthy role model for a new generation.

Personally, I feel so privileged to have spent this last year immersed in the worlds of these seventeen brilliant and unique storytellers, to foster a spirit of community and to draw them together for this book. Through essays, poems and memoir, they explore themes of identity, connection, disconnection, food, rejection, relationships, history, art, love . . . there's a universality to their experiences, even if the stories themselves are beautifully unique. We are taken onto hospital battle grounds, discover the lasting effects when a Caucasian relative deliberately whitens skin tone in a portrait, and uncover the culture of television and film casting for Asians. We ask what it's like to be East and Southeast Asian in Britain through the lens of the pandemic, and interrogate the way Asian women are 'seen' or rather *not* seen, in being conflated with other races, erased and sexualised. I want these stories to challenge your expectations, be troubling, be illuminating, resonate. I want them to sit with you for a long time, be recurrently thought about and shift world-views.

The anthology is by no means meant to be exhaustive – I'm aware that there are ethnicities and subjects that I've not been able to include. There are many more experiences that need to be brought to light, and stories that need to be told. But my hope is that this book is the beginning of a conversation that will only grow bigger, and will enrich your lives as much as it has so far mine.

Once Upon a Time in . . . Middlesex

Helena Lee

'The Orient is not only adjacent to Europe; it is also
the place of Europe's greatest and richest and oldest
colonies, the source of its civilizations and languages,
its cultural contestant, and one of its deepest and
most recurring images of the Other.'
     – Edward Said, *Introduction to Orientalism* (1977)

My mother never told me what it was to be like me, a 'BBC'
– not British, mind you, but British Born Chinese.

My mother had a telephone voice, which was posher than
her normal voice. It was the more pronounced 'T's and 'D's
that gave it away. Only later, when friends would say: 'I
didn't know your mum was foreign,' meaning 'not from
round here', did I realise that she didn't sound British. She
was born in what was then Malaya in the city of Ipoh, the
capital of the state of Perak. Ipoh was known for two things,
she said, beautiful bean sprouts and beautiful women, which
seemed, although self-congratulatory, reasonable to me. The

stories she wove from her childhood were threaded with the otherworldliness of the extraordinary – malevolent spirits, crocodiles, a stepfather who had supposedly been kidnapped by the Japanese occupation – but she left that all behind when she was twenty to study in what she considered the motherland: Britain, drawn to the literature, the temperate weather and the lack of mosquitoes. I had the impression that the Malaysians loved the British, even if they were not supposed to (yes, they might have colonised the Straits, but look at the order and freedom they bestowed!). China hardly got a mention, perhaps because she was several generations removed from the country. Britain, on the other hand, was seen as a place of steadfast opportunity. The British allowed her to come and live with them and she felt at home. So much so that she met a man in St Albans from another colony, Hong Kong, and married him. He became my father. No wonder she liked it here.

When I was growing up it seemed perfectly easy to be like everyone else. After all, I sounded like them in the classroom (with that non-distinguishable accent that wasn't like anyone's from *EastEnders* or *Coronation Street*). I had kiss-chase and hopscotch friends, lived in a suburb of north London and rode hand-me-down bikes that cranked down long streets. I went to birthday parties where we jammed on hats and gloves and hacked at bars of Dairy Milk with knives and forks; my restaurant of choice was Pizza Hut, in which I loaded up on bacon bits from the unlimited salad bar and hoped the formidably big Care Bears with fur greasy from pawing toddlers would entertain us. I read voraciously, and loved traipsing down to Foyles bookshop, a place of joyful disorder, to pick up another Roald Dahl classic. I climbed trees where I could, because that was what it was to be wholesome. My mother and I would chat to the Jewish neighbours from Czechoslovakia, spend Saturdays in Brent Cross shopping centre and treat ourselves to M&S prawn cocktail sandwiches at 12 o'clock. Wasn't that what it was to be British?

Every now and then, something would pop this British bubble of mine – the times of inexplicable exclusion when I just didn't get the joke. Like the word 'fart' or other scato-logical terms that were bandied around the playground like plastic footballs. In actuality, I did know what these words meant. It's just that I knew them in Cantonese. My mother had so adopted what she saw as the British attribute of modesty that she refused to say these words in English.

From then on, I began to see what else I'd not been told. The more Enid Blyton stories I read, the more friends' houses I went round to, the more it became clear that our rituals were not the same as my blue-eyed, blonde-haired best friend Michelle's. Her family feasted on turkey at Christmas, just not stuffed with soy sauce and glutinous rice. My evenings were taken up with piano and violin practice (I would typic-ally run scales forty times every night) while Michelle acquired badges from Brownies. My mother taught me the currencies and capital cities of major countries, and asked me to repeat my times tables forwards – and backwards – in my spare time. I remember one particularly traumatic Bank Holiday during which my father made me watch *The Last Emperor* when I should really have been catching up on the latest episode of *Neighbours*. And then there was the time I was shouted at for gripping my chopsticks 'like dead people' – a technique apparently less favoured in the Chinese community. I'd wager that Michelle had never lost confidence in her fork-holding skills.

I stopped using chopsticks. I refused dim sum. I clamoured for McDonald's cheeseburgers and spaghetti bolognese. I stayed away from the phone when my father's mother *Ma Ma* called from Hong Kong because I was required to speak in Cantonese.

One day I came home from Chinese school, which was every Saturday morning, and started my homework. Out came the pen, out came the notebook of wide squares, each one about to be filled with a character meaningless to me. *Shǒu Shǒu Shǒu Shǒu Shǒu Shǒu*. Practising the Chinese strokes, repeatedly etching them, I worked from top to bottom, and I began to cry.

Why was I doing something that so forcibly differentiated myself from everyone else, learning a language that hindered rather than helped my communication with those I wanted to be with? Why was I immersing myself in a culture that separated me from my friends? Who were these other people in Chinese school – for whom school on a Saturday made sense? They were Chinese. It was their first language. It wasn't mine.

I left Chinese school and I never went back. I gave up the idea of becoming a hot-shot violinist, or a medical practitioner. I didn't want to be held up as a paragon in my family in the way every Chinese parent I knew did with their genius doctor-progeny.

I look back at the decisions I made. I thought it was about my own happiness, but it was my way of surviving my immediate environment. In the 1980s, there were no cool Asian subcultures or figureheads for me to cling on to – after all, if China was a brand, then it was synonymous with cheaply made goods, martial arts, and MSG. I wanted to prove to those around me that I could be as British as they were. At sixth form, I was introduced to Classics, and eventually went on to study the subject at Oxford University. I decided to learn Ancient Greek and Latin from scratch while I was there, so that I could understand the literature, philosophy and ideas at the heart of Western civilisation, but also to immerse myself in an area that was not expected of me, to strike out on my own, to do my thing. How telling. Could I have chosen a better subject that so clearly disregarded my heritage? How had I acquired such a distorted world-view?

In retrospect, I understand that these decisions were about a yearning for acceptance, rather than celebrating and embracing my difference, because no one else seemed to be experiencing that difference. I was distancing myself away from that convention of what Chinese immigrants were supposed to do, and that suited me fine.

And in the process, I have been guilty of perpetuating stereotypes, been apologetic for my culture. I've used the term 'Tiger parenting' as a shortcut to explain my proficiency at playing the piano aged three. But I was never comfortable with this inexcusable self-deprecation. I realise how reductive I was in branding my mother a 'Tiger mum', and how dismissive I had been of her own achievements as a parent. I was writing off her own cultural journey, her way of imbuing me with a love of education, literature and learning. Her experience is to be lauded, not belittled.

There is a danger in the preservation of silence, in assuming that the experiences of previous generations exist in isolation. In my wider family, there is an unwillingness to reflect, to share, to pass on the wisdom gained from any sort of struggle. Instead, filial piety dictates that by virtue of being older, parents should be respected. Children should know their place. To question our elders – their actions, their judgement – amounts to transgression of the family structure. In turn, shame is a powerful emotion that all Chinese families would like to avoid. We would do well to forget the poverty of our youth and the achievement of social mobility. The American Dream would be anathema to the notion of Chinese success. When prodded on unearthing home truths about my father's childhood in Hong Kong and my grandfather's multiple spouses, one uncle refused to be drawn in: 'Why do you want to talk about the bad times?' he said with impatience. 'We should focus on the future.' The implication being that of course success has always defined our story.

But we underestimate the fluidity of these experiences, how the effects trickle down from person to person. It's only in asking questions now that I am starting to understand the context I was brought up in. It's only now that my mother has told me about the lack of opportunity she would have faced had she stayed in Malaysia, both as a woman, and as a descendant of Chinese immigrants. Her grandparents had faced starvation and left Hokchiu in the Fujian Province in the early 20th century to settle in Sitiawan on the west coast of the Malay peninsula. My grandmother, the elegant and reserved Madame Yew Eng Lan, was twice widowed and had been left with six children to support by her early forties. She had precious little time to spend with her brood, focused as she was on keeping the family afloat by dealing in stocks and shares. There was no extra money for further education, which was reserved for the Malays and the prosperous. And there was an added complication: as my mother had been premature – two pounds when she was born – her father had believed that she brought his business bad luck and had beaten her as a young child, and as the daughter of Eng Lan's unloved second husband, my mother failed to receive the maternal affection and support that she craved. Her prospects were bleak indeed.

And so, when she left school, she answered an advert from the NHS looking to sponsor those in the Commonwealth to become nurses. In 1971, she boarded a Caledonian

Airways plane for her first ever flight. Five stops, a prolonged fainting spell, and twenty-four hours later, she arrived in England, knowing, she says, that she would not go back.

What seems intrepid today was simply necessity. The year she arrived, she met my father – who was also studying – abandoned her ambition to become a nurse and decided to pursue accountancy.

They were first-generation immigrants. Cultural difference defined their lives. They were also Anglophiles, but not English, the 'other' in many senses (my paternal grandmother stopped speaking to my father for marrying a woman from Malaysia rather than China). In fact, they had to create their own ecosystem that was particular to them – one that didn't even have the benefit of familiarity of coming from the same country. They had little money and a thirst for education. Independence was the goal of their endeavours – and endeavour they did, despite the name-calling, hardships and racism. The diploma in civil engineering from Hatfield Polytechnic – my father's ticket to giving up the three jobs he'd been holding down – was a small victory. My parents moved from a room with no central heating, in which they cooked all their meals in a rice cooker, to a leaky squat in Hatfield that was so damp that my new-born brother was drenched in water as he lay in his cot. It was a significant moment when they were granted a council house. A garden! Three bedrooms! All their possessions fitted into two suitcases, so they furnished their lodgings with a bed from the Co-op and second-hand kitchen chairs that they bought for a pound each.

They had no blueprints for marriage, or parenthood, or how to forge a life in Britain. Drawing together a skeleton community – a cousin here, a colleague there – they collected not just friends who spoke Cantonese, but those who, like them, were new to the country: Italians, Iraqis, Americans, Czechs. There was the Irish butcher my mother had befriended, who took pity on them because they couldn't afford to buy food for Christmas. He roasted a whole bird for them, which they lived off for two weeks (and might explain why they decided to jazz Christmases up with glutinous rice stuffing).

In keeping this from me, how could I appreciate their trajectory? All I saw were patchworks of traditions that were never quite right (why were laksas made with tinned pilchards? Why did my father insist on noisily slurping his noodles in front of my friends?). Equally, where was my curiosity about that elusive past, preferring instead to think that it had ever been thus, that we were somehow entitled to a normal, middle-class existence?

I see now that immigration is an act of creativity. In leaving behind the warmth of those familiar societal structures in Malaysia, in Hong Kong, in searching for a better life, my parents opened themselves up to the unknown. Divorced from the circumstances of their birth, they had that unquestioning drive to build, to focus on progress and the present, rather than the uphill journey of their past – a journey that I was unaware of until I had a daughter of my own, a journey that can surely be found in every family's story. I am now a mother of two, conscious that my girls have this cultural inheritance running through their veins. And so I encourage my parents to illuminate those previously lost years, keen to pass on the wisdom learnt from their extraordinary past, so that my daughters can look closer to home for their role models. Remarkably, my mother and father have taken up the mantle, and are themselves questioning their siblings, looking for answers. I've come to accept that although their style of parenting was at times dictatorial, it was to help me understand what it was to be Chinese; just so that I would not forget where I came from. It doesn't matter that my mother didn't fill in the gaps nor tell me exactly how to be a BBC. The more I was told, the less I would have learnt, because my parents had stood for something different. But I like being different, and that the generations before me fought to be different. Of all the legacies I can inherit, I'm proud that it's this one.

The White Series

Mary Jean Chan

White (I)

During the early days of the pandemic, she asked herself if language meant anything, when it was so clearly the body that faced an existential threat. Keep going, she told her body. One day, she began losing blood. Her period lasted for thirty days. It was the month lockdown ended in the UK, when people flew off on European holidays. Stress, her father once told her, can make you ill. It can make your hair turn white. She looked in the mirror that evening and saw many silvery strands sprouting, like dandelions. The worst thing about the pandemic, she confessed to her partner as they lay in bed, is that other people – no matter how much I love them – are all potential hosts. Each night, she would dream about being in a large room full of people, then realise that she did not have her mask on, that everyone was unmasked. In the dream, intimacy became an interminable threat. Bodies became repugnant. It was in 2003 when she first learnt how droplets – breathed gently into air – could kill. They called it SARS. As a thirteen-year-old, she learnt this term alongside other words, like sacrifice, sacred, scared.

White (II)
after Sara Ahmed

On my weekly train to Oxford, whiteness greets me as a bad habit, a kind of stopping device. I cease to drink from my orange juice as two white men sit opposite me. I try not to assume anything, to continue to inhabit a space of equals. One of them speaks. All those Chinese tourists who go to Bicester, he murmurs. You can go into a lift there and hear more than three languages these days, makes you wonder whether you're in England at all. His companion laughs and nods. I stare at my iPhone, sip my juice for strength. Perhaps my face is a sign they cannot – have chosen not to – read. From my bag, I produce a book of poems, placing it in the white space between us. The man glances at me. There is a look in his eyes I cannot help but recognise. He pauses, turns the conversation elsewhere.

White (III)

I learnt that English meant good, that good meant the satisfaction of being praised, if only for one bright school day. For twelve years, I was taught that English was the lingua franca. Imagine being taught to revere a language from the age of six, when children are most willing to please. Prior to 1997, French was an elective of equal standing to Cantonese. A rumour went around the school that prefects used to patrol the grounds, fining students if they ever spoke to one another in their mother tongue. English at all times, the teachers trilled. I never chose English: English was thrust upon me. My native fluency in English was a political outcome, wrought from the skeins of colonisation, Christian missionary work and language policing. Later, I fell in love with English of my own accord. Or did I? Love, when socially accepted, becomes habit. I took home the English Literature prize for three years in a row, would let no one else come close. It became a badge of honour, a symbol of my uniqueness, though I was lonelier than I had ever been. At times, English feels like the best kind of evening light. On other days, English becomes something harder, like a white shield. It occurs to me now that sword and word are only one letter apart.

Mistaken for Strangers

Sharlene Teo

In November 2019, my then-partner was showing me something on his phone when he scrolled past what I thought was a dimly lit picture of me.

'Wait, what's that?' I asked.

'Nothing,' he said.

Intrigued, I made him scroll back.

The image depicted an Asian girl with long hair in a dark room who resembled me at first glance. Upon closer scrutiny, I'd mistaken a stranger for myself. Racial impression elided individuality, for the callous moment it takes someone in an office, classroom, or wider social group to call one Asian girl loudly by the very different name of an entirely different person of the same ethnicity.

'That's M,' my then-partner, who is white, said sheepishly, referring to a friend of his I'd never met, a 'tiny Japanese-American woman' (his words, not mine) he claimed to have befriended through basketball practice.

'When did you take this?' I asked.

'Last week.'

'You didn't mention that you met up,' I said, feeling unpleasantly like a possessive, haranguing girlfriend.

It transpired, after a lot of arguing, that all the time we'd been exclusively together, he had been dating M secretly. They hadn't met through basketball practice after all, a detail I'd always been sceptical about due to the uncharacteristic and surprising choice of sport as well as the cagey and shifting verbiage with which he told the story. The real story, it turned out, was that he met her via the dating app Happn, which he'd previously mentioned never having tried. He claimed it 'wasn't physical cheating' and that he had 'emotional issues' that made him covertly meet up with M whenever he felt bored or particularly lonely because she lived in the same postcode and it was convenient. Unable to accept those explanations, I broke up with him.

Would it have hurt a little less if M wasn't also Asian? If I hadn't found out by the icky, accidental revelation of that photo I'd mistaken for myself, that moment of identification turned to confusion turned to alienation? The short answer is yes.

It is one thing to feel like you are not enough for someone, and another to feel like you are entirely interchangeable. The myth of the model minority perpetuates a narrative of exceptional socioeconomic success, skill and attainment in order to justify one's position in society. If you work hard enough and prove yourself, maybe you won't be expendable.

I messaged M on Instagram in a fit of pique, and in case she didn't know about me.

Sneaking around with someone's boyfriend is not cool. It's on him, but you are a terrible person too.

Quite understandably, she blocked me.

The word 'happen' derives from the Old English noun 'hap' meaning 'chance, a person's luck, fortune, fate'; also, 'unforeseen occurrence'. There's nothing undeliberate about downloading a dating app, although there is something chancy about who you'll be attracted to and who you'll hit it off with.

Twenty or thirty years ago people would speak in almost supernaturally analogue terms of fate or luck bringing them together, serendipitous real-life encounters. Nowadays, due to a wider social shift toward digital dependency, romantic and sexual encounters are commonly mediated through technology. And therein lies the exhausting possibility, the algorithm-sanctioned multiplicity of modern romance.

Nowadays, dating apps have anodyne, tinkly names like Happn, Bumble and Hinge, as if to ameliorate the complex and oftentimes unconscious and unconscionable ways in which we decide who we do and do not want to date or sleep with.

What are the odds in England of a white man dating two or three Asian women in a row, and what does it imply about him?

What are the odds in England of an Asian woman dating

two or three white men in a row, and what does it imply about her?

Whether down to preference, fetish, or happenstance, the sexual politics are not the same nor simple to articulate.

Moving from Singapore to the UK fourteen years ago for my undergraduate law degree, I soon grew accustomed to explaining to English people that Singapore wasn't a part of China, and that China, Japan and Korea weren't the only countries in Asia. I'd moved halfway across the world naively expecting campus life to be a haven of liberal acceptance and open-mindedness, my head filled with rose-tinted visions of students from different nationalities sitting together under trees (!) having edifying and in no way insufferable discussions about philosophy and literature. I don't even know which books or movies I got that idea from except I was sorely mistaken.

In my first year of university, unless we were obliterating our inhibitions with alcohol in the student union, everyone seemed as shy and nervous as I was. Within the Law faculty, people stuck mostly to their stratum. During lectures, the toothy blonde girls from Chelsea in their Ugg boots and ski society hoodies were just as exotic to me as the dewy-skinned princesses from Hong Kong who sat in the back row being worshipped by their spiky-haired, Comme des Garçons-wearing boyfriends who were also from Hong Kong. Despite some macroeconomic similarities between Singapore and Hong Kong (both former British colonies, as well as regional financial centres highly dependent on trade, with majority Chinese populations), the glamorous couples from Hong Kong were just as foreign to me as the students from Ghana, Poland, or Brazil. Even though, to non-Asians, we 'all looked the same', geographic proximity and shared Chinese ancestry was no more a guarantee of mutual understanding and rapport than one's horoscope or birth chart. Sure, sometimes it worked out, and some people believed in it, but as an abiding social assumption it was dicey.

In a memorable scene from the 2004 film *Mean Girls*, kohl-eyed iconoclast Janis Ian breaks down the cliques of North Shore High to new girl Cady Heron. 'You got your freshmen, ROTC guys, preps, JV jocks,' Janis explains. 'Asian nerds,' she drawls, as the screen fades into a bird's-eye view of a cafeteria table filled with East Asian boys. 'Cool Asians,' she continues, as the camera pans to the next table where a tanned, sexy girl with long hair takes centre stage, lifting her turquoise shirt and pointing to her belly button piercing. Those clique titles are reflective of the biting, culturally insensitive humour of Hollywood teen comedies from the early 2000s, with regressive stereotypes such as 'girls who eat their feelings' and 'girls who don't eat anything'. But it was the distinction between 'Asian nerds' and 'Cool Asians', categories that seemed both sweeping and limiting all at once, that stuck with me. Popular culture plays an undeniable role in shaping our perceptions, and without adequate representation, it felt like Asians who didn't fall into either the nerdy or cool designations had little social value.

Stuck somewhere in between, in a foreign country where I felt constantly pigeonholed for my own foreignness, I tried to avoid interrogating my own identity. Instead, I decided to play up its modalities. In first-year seminars, I affected the trope of the reticent Asian (like Lilly Onakuramara, the harmful caricature of a near-mute Asian savant from the 2012 film *Pitch Perfect*) barely speaking all term because I was terrified and also because I'd realised I hated what I was studying. I felt like Law was just people looking for loopholes to get away with doing bad things, or setting over-long, fusty precedents for what was and wasn't a bad thing. Out of the classroom I smoked Camel Lights and sought refuge in the Canadian indie music that was popular at the time, as well as contemporary fiction and poetry that was a panacea for the intolerable dryness of my legal text-books. I wrote sad poems and short stories set in Singapore, fabulist vignettes framed in a hazy, humid environment that felt unthreatening and familiar to me. At the end of the year I cut all my hair off, dyeing it a graphic and unflattering blue that telegraphed my uniqueness, that said: look at me! I'm not like those girls from Hong Kong who wear high heels in the snow and only hang out with their boyfriends; I have fellow Asian and Singaporean friends too, but I have friends from all over, I'm *alternative,* and *international*.

I was trying to impress everyone-who-wasn't-like-me, but predominantly white people, in a bid to assimilate myself into my new environment. There was something more insidi-ous at work too, like the beginnings of a flesh-eating disease;

a form of racialised self-loathing and constant comparison with other Asian women on campus that I didn't know the slightest thing about, either never measuring up to their invincible prettiness, their superiority and composure, or tearing them down through snap judgements in order to make myself feel better. Asian women felt just as unknowable as everyone else, but not entirely unlike me, and therein lay my discomfort, my petty bone to pick. We were part of a sisterhood, in a sense, united by how white people got us mixed up or made assumptions about the vague Far East we came from. We were compatriots in a structure of oppression, but instead of camaraderie I felt threatened into a defensive competitiveness, a childish desire to attest my individuality.

I was spring-cleaning recently when I found an old photograph of me and my two best friends from university. S was a British Asian woman of Gujarati descent, wise-cracking, wild-haired and brilliant. O was a former punk from Hong Kong. He played the drums and had an encyclopaedic knowledge of world cinema and sociological theory. Amongst other things, we bonded over a shared feeling of otherness and not knowing quite where we belonged nor how we wanted to be labelled or defined, if at all. Come to think of it, people might have thought O and I were a couple – we were inseparable around campus and at parties. I might very well have come across as a girl from Hong Kong who wore high heels in the snow and only hung out with her boyfriend. Who knows? After graduation, over time, S and I drifted apart and eventually fell out of contact. O moved back to Hong Kong and then to South Korea, where he still lives with his pet cat.

But in the photograph we are all together, sitting side-by-side on someone's sofa at a house party. O is holding a biscuit in front of his face, ironically pouting at the camera. S has her trademark messy hair and a canny smile playing on her mouth. I am caught mid-laugh, wearing a bohemian headband that was trendy in 2009 and woefully passé now. The three of us look so young, so unmistakably at ease with each other and unmistakably ourselves.

In his 1903 book *The Souls of Black Folk*, W.E.B. Du Bois defines double consciousness as 'the sense of always looking at one's self through the eyes of others'. Du Bois originated the concept to apply to the African-American experience of the early 1900s, describing how the internalisation of anti-Black racism from the outside world shaped and damaged Black people's self-perception and made it difficult for them to reconcile different components of their identity. In Singapore, I had the privilege of being the ethnic majority. I'd grown up sympathising with but not truly understanding what it felt like for my Indian and Malay friends to have their selfhood sidelined, belittled or glossed over altogether in casual conversation. In school, I remember how common-place racist jokes were about Malays and Indians. How for them to call someone out was to be seen as lacking in humour, being over-sensitive. In England, suddenly cast in the position of a minority, I had a bitter taste of what that felt like. And it also became apparent to me that my self-othering and the pressure I felt to perform or refute an identity imposed upon me by the white, Western gaze hadn't sprung out of nowhere.

Growing up in Singapore in the 1990s and 2000s, colonialism cast a long, persistent shadow over the education system and media; from the imposition of English as our lingua franca, to the Englishmen who dominated our literature syllabus. Local beauty magazines featured mostly Eurasian models on the covers, gorgeous women who toed that fashionably ambiguous line between whiteness and exoticism; if any Chinese models appeared, they flaunted the kind of supermodel symmetry and unattainable poise of pageant queens and starlets from Taiwan, China or Hong Kong. Newspapers advertised slimming treatments, getting wrapped in clingfilm to shed fat. Space-age machines that zapped scars and stretch marks away. Whitening creams that stripped the melanin off you. In school, my classmates worshipped Korean or Japanese pop stars – girl-women with bleached flaxen hair, so doe-eyed and ethereal they seemed untouched by corporeal realities such as sweating or acne.

Had I grown up in contention with a kind of idealised Pan-Asian woman who didn't exist, airbrushed of any troublesome signifiers of contradiction or particularity? I am particular but nothing special. I am an ethnically Chinese person who can't even speak fluent Chinese. I am a Singaporean person who is sick of white people telling me

I speak such good English or getting me confused for another Asian writer at literary events. Misspelling and changing my very short surname 'Teo' to 'Tao' because it is more legibly foreign to them; it all sounds the same, anyway. Being a Singaporean is such a vital part of who I am, and I am proud of where I come from. But I don't want to live in Singapore any more, the site of childhood, what is past for me. I prefer to live in England, the imperfect present, even though I don't identify as English, and being a foreigner here has its attendant discomforts. I frequently feel like I don't belong in either country, like I'm failing between two cultures, two temporal modes of being.

Every so often, Facebook informs me that it's so-and-so's birthday, or someone is getting married. For a split second I can't place the stranger in the profile picture, before memory filters in and I recognise the person from my college or secondary school. It's a matter-of-fact wonder to spectate, across the distance of a screen, all these people who you last saw at the age of sixteen or eighteen grown up and beaming in wedding photos, or cradling babies.

Sometimes I think about how different my life would have turned out if I'd never left Singapore. I wonder whether I'd be writing books or doing something else. If I'd be married with kids of my own, what our living room would look like. I think, also, about how being a minority has inflected my attitudes toward dating and relationships. In *Minor Feelings: A Reckoning on Race and the Asian Condition,*

Cathy Park Hong writes that 'the Asian woman is reminded every day that her attractiveness is a perversion, in instances ranging from skin-crawling Tinder messages ("I'd like to try my first Asian woman") to microaggressions from white friends.' Hong describes how friends never failed to warn her 'if a white guy was attracted to me, that he probably had an Asian fetish. The result: I distrusted my desirousness. My sexuality was a pathology. If anyone non-Asian liked me, there was something wrong with him.'

I felt this for the first time when I was twenty. I was in a bookshop in London when a white man who looked like he was in his forties approached me and asked if I'd read any works by Haruki Murakami.

I mumbled in the affirmative and continued browsing the display table.

'Are you from Japan?' the man enquired.

I shook my head and affected a brief smile before breaking eye contact.

'Korea?' he asked. I could feel his eyes on me, scrutinising, profiling. 'China? Vietnam? Thailand?'

'Singapore. I'm from Singapore,' I replied, finally. I don't remember how I ended the conversation, except that it left me feeling exhausted and frankly, undesirably, angry.

This conversation comes up over and over, in various places. Sometimes I let the men continue until they run out of Asian countries they know by heart. Sometimes their voices — so hopeful at Japan! — sound audibly deflated as they go along. I've learnt the hard way to stay neutral and bear it. Not to retaliate sarcastically. Once, a man followed me down the platform at Paddington station chanting '*ni hao ma, konnichiwa*, sexy, sexy' and I told him to get lost – only for him to start shouting and running after me. It was terrifying.

What's the harm in curiosity, however misplaced? The problem with someone guessing where a 'foreign-looking' person is from without any basis of interaction is the implicit assumption that racialised optics and otherness form their totality. That there's nothing more to a person than the patina of exoticism. White men 'guessing' the ethnic origins of Asian women carries a great deal of historical and cultural baggage, from Yellow Peril to the colonial-era- and Second World War-propagated sexual stereotype of the exotic and submissive Oriental Woman.

As a teenager in Singapore, I dated Singaporean Chinese boys. In England, I've dated mostly white men, not out of a particular preference but because white people make up 87.2 per cent of the total population and by extension the majority of the dating pool. I would love to fall in love with someone who shares similar attitudes and fascinations with me and has a lived understanding of growing up in an Asian household and the minority experience; but it simply hasn't happened. Not only would that be amazing, but it would also make my parents very happy.

Feel-good bromides such as 'you like who you like' don't account for the sinking in my chest when I second-guess whether a non-Asian person only likes me because they have an Asian fetish. The influential nineteenth-century psychiatrist Richard von Krafft-Ebing defines fetishism as 'the association of lust with the idea of certain portions of the female person, or with certain articles of female attire . . . in pathological eroticism the fetish itself (rather than the person associated with it) becomes the exclusive object of sexual desire.' Being fetishised isn't flattering because it's intensely depersonalising. Instead of being seen as a full and complex being, the fetish object is held as just that – an object, a flat, reflective surface on which fantasies of docile, quirky or sexy otherness are projected.

Not everyone is a fetishist, of course, and oftentimes curiosity is well-intentioned. And the judgement cuts both ways. In Singapore, there's a derogatory term for Singaporean Chinese women who seem to date only white men – Sarong Party Girls, a term anecdotally derived from colonial times when local women who wore sarongs were invited to British military soirées. We can't control how we are perceived by others, but we can control the assumptions we make about other people.

At heart, everyone craves real kindness in a world so often starved and sceptical of it. Small, unshowy acts of grace that translate beyond language and social status. Moments of micro-compassion and genuine warmth seem rarer than ever in an increasingly divided, judgemental and paranoid global climate. Every human being, regardless of ethnicity, just wants to be truly witnessed. Rigid constructions of gender and race severely limit our ways of seeing each other and being expansively, generously human. A woman's age is so much more than just fuckable and unfuckable, functional and redundant. Any age at all is precious time spent embodying the aliveness we are gifted with from babyhood until some slow or sudden end.

Since the start of the pandemic in 2020 and the resulting prevalence of terming Covid as the 'Wuhan virus' or 'Chinese virus', anti-Asian racism has spiked dramatically in the US and UK. In light of the horrifying news of the Atlanta shootings in which six of the eight people killed were women of Asian descent, and the grim news stories of violence against Asian men and women that pop up with increasing regularity, it feels dangerous for Asian people to even just try to get by and feel safe.

Microaggressions and unconscious biases against the Asian community are being discussed as if this is a recent occurrence and not part of a longstanding pattern of stereotyping and socio-culturally categorising Asian people. Whether regarded as Cool Asians or Nerdy Asians, Quiet Asians or Smart Asians, the myth of Asians as well-behaved model minorities perpetuates a long and casual history of Asian discrimination.

Ordering Asian food from menus printed in wonton font, an ethnic typeface, expresses a generic Asianness. Pick and choose. Pad Thai or sushi or laksa today? Asian food is nice, Asian countries are nice for a holiday! Party in the expat area! You can't fit it in a carousel post, you can't fit it in a hashtag. All the ways we are erased.

Why are Asian slurs social canon? On the streets, some men call out 'konnichiwa' or 'ni hao ma' with gleeful self-satisfaction, as if every Asian girl is an exotic pet obliged to respond to this racialised greeting, this violent lack of recognition. I think of that man who chased me down the train platform, his leering turned to outrage at my mild retaliation. I think of the other man in the bookshop almost fifteen years ago, incredulous that I already knew who the famous literary author Haruki Murakami was, disappointed that I wasn't Japanese, the Asian ethnicity he'd either pigeon-holed me as or somehow hoped I would be. I wonder if those men even remember these incidents with a stranger from years ago. Somehow, I don't think so. I think memory only retains what is tethered in emotion, guilt, exception. I don't think either of those interactions seemed in any way exceptional to them, in any way harmful. I can imagine the men rationalising that I, the little Asian girl, should have felt flattered by any attention. I can imagine some people arguing that if I don't want strangers to be racist to me, I should go back to where I came from, or stop complaining.

Where are you really from? implies: you don't belong here.

Me love you long time implies: I shame you all the time. If we retaliate, we're told *It's just a joke! Lighten up! Political correctness, it's gone mad these days.*

Madame Butterfly. Almond-shaped eyes. The flutter of a

fan. Wartime honey. Gap year honey is a continuation of the same. It is not 'flattering', this pattern of inattention, it is flattening instead. Flattening a whole person into a fetish object, a collector's item. Yellow fever as servile innuendo, as punchline: ironic racism is still racism. Not laughing with, laughing at. It's not funny. Second-guessing desirability as an aberration. An Asian fetish is more than just a harmless preference, it's a hangover of imperialism. Deliberate othering: imbalanced, sustained. To say Oriental like a rug or an ornament, to say Oriental as casual racism trussed up in culture, gilded in nostalgia for the older, whiter days. Back when Asian people were too frightened to complain. These days we're still scared, still hurt and tired, but desperate – and maybe just a little hopeful – for change.

Portraits

Claire Kohda

It was a cold day. I sat in the back on the drive over. My mum had a container of mini doughnuts on her lap. She passed me one. 'Eat as many as you can because they won't offer us food,' she said. I looked out of the window and imagined myself transported out of my own body and into the bodies of the people we passed, adults roaming around freely, some with kebabs or fish and chips, waiting to cross roads, taking dogs for walks, umbrellas up, or running with hair soaked. Those were the people I wanted to be – the people not visiting their nans and granddads.

Parked outside Nan and Granddad's terraced house was a trailer on which a few boys played. My nan and granddad didn't like these boys; their parents were never around and so they entertained themselves by throwing cat poo and snails into my nan's flowerbeds. When we arrived, they stopped their playing and glared at us as we walked from our car to the front door and while we waited for Nan and Granddad to answer. If only I could use those glares as a rope to escape into one of the boys' brains for a bit, just so that I could skip this visit and then rejoin my parents for the journey back home.

We rang the doorbell. I hoped that they wouldn't be in. But they were always in, because my dad had called ahead of time, and because they were always in. Through the frosted glass the shape of Granddad became visible, and then it opened the door. We went inside. Into the entrance hall, through the dining room, then into the living room. Large sofas with floral, tapestry-like upholstery, tables under which were smaller and smaller tables, with one tiny and useless table right in the centre. Bright white lace coasters. A grandfather clock against the wall that made several noises – a ticking, a clicking, a whirr, and a cuckoo sound.

On that day, Nan was sitting on one of the armchairs, dressed all in white as always, her hair dyed a golden blonde. Her dog Jasper – a Cavalier King Charles – greeted us. 'Hello, Jasper,' I said. Jasper padded away. We went to the cupboard where Granddad ceremoniously waited for us and handed him our coats one by one. Granddad hung them on hangers and closed the cupboard behind us. We filed back into the living area, in our usual order – Mum first, me second, Dad last – and sat down in our usual places on the two-seater sofa, with me squished in the middle. Ahead of us, the gas fire was on, imitating real fire. Around it were fake stones made of plaster that were supposed to give the impression that this little terraced house was a cottage and had charm. The TV was on very loud. Nan was watching

EastEnders. 'Hello,' she said – and she smiled towards my dad. 'How's work, Paul?'

'Oh,' I felt my dad shuffling in his seat next to me. Dad is an artist, a point of contention for his parents – and if not contention, then of bemusement at the very least. 'Well, I . . .'

My mind wandered. My nan and granddad's house represented, to me, the extreme end of the Englishness in my family. Although I hadn't visited Japan since I was four, I imagined that there must be the equivalent – something pure and incorruptibly Japanese – in our family there too: maybe the house of a very old relative who wore kimonos whenever she went outside, tatami mats on the floor, a little Shinto shrine, plum blossom incense – where I would feel just as out of place as I felt in my nan and granddad's house. I was neither Japanese nor English in my mind. And, so, in my nan and granddad's house – the house in which rice and pizza were considered too foreign – I often daydreamed, as though my mind wouldn't stick to the reality around me.

I watched, for a moment, as a bald man on TV angrily shoved past an older woman, and someone called after him. I watched my nan's eyes steal a quick glance at the screen while my dad continued talking. Above, the ceiling fan slowly spun, casting large shadows. All along the mantlepiece were figurines of different dogs. A collie, a Labrador, Cavalier King Charleses. On the walls were several photographs. There were a few of all the different dogs they'd had as pets; there was Nan and Granddad – at their wedding,

I think; my dad and his brother. There were some pictures of my cousins, too. I looked at the clock; its pendulum seemed to swing very slowly. And then my mum said something to me quietly in Japanese. It was something that came with a nudge in the ribs. 'Ku-re-a,' I heard, the way my mum pronounces my name. I refocused my attention. There was a painting out on Nan's lap. 'Ku-re-a, go look at it,' my mum said to me in Japanese again. I stood up as Granddad came in with tea. There, with my family surrounding me, I could see I was a mix of them all, while looking like none of them.

'Aha!' Granddad said, looking at the painting. 'Your mum's painting,' he said to Dad. Granddad set down three cups of tea on coasters with pictures of dogs on them on one of the small tables. My dad's had too much milk as usual. My mum's was too weak. Mine was sugary, because 'children like sweet things'. Granddad sat down on the other armchair and turned his attention towards the TV.

I don't remember what happened next. My memory of this moment is a still image, as though my brain quickly took a photo of the scene and then escaped, not knowing how to comprehend it properly. In the image, I see a canvas of around 30 x 40cm. On it is me, painted in acrylics. I am smiling. I am wearing green, my school uniform. I can tell I've been painted from my school photograph. But I look strange. My hair is a lighter brown than its actual colour – which is a shade that is almost black. The irises of my eyes are not the yellowy-brown they are but something much

42

lighter; my eyebrows are light brown, thin and shaped, rather than black, thick and unruly as they were then; and my skin is porcelain-white, with a beautiful, soft English-rose blush.

I vaguely remember my dad saying something, but I don't remember what. It was a kind and encouraging remark about the brushstrokes. My mum was speaking, too – and I remember I felt especially aware of her Japanese accent as she did, perhaps because the version of me in the painting was like a version of me with no Japanese heritage; a version of me born not to my mum but to a different woman, who was more in line with the person my grandparents might have expected their son to marry.

I don't know what I said to my nan, but I would have said something nice. Any quietness while I was a child was attributed to the fact that I was very shy, so no one would have noticed if I didn't seem to like the painting. Although, I don't think I necessarily didn't like it as such. It was just confusing, and difficult to comprehend. It was like looking into a mirror that showed just half of me; it was like looking into a mirror that showed me what, at the time, I had wanted to be, which was completely white and not Japanese at all.

I don't remember a time when a version of me didn't exist in paint. My dad first painted me before I was born. In an oil and acrylic painting, my mum rests with her eyes closed, wearing a pair of dungarees; I am inside her pregnant belly, which sits beneath her clasped hands – a few strokes of yellow, peach and black. Soon after that, when I was nine months old, my dad started to sketch me; in between lines of handwriting describing his process of learning a few Japanese words are drawings of me in ink and watercolour. In one picture, I'm asleep under the word '*oyasuminasai*' (goodnight); in another, I'm hitting a small Japanese drum with a plastic stick. In 1994, my dad drew me in charcoal; I'm at a table and my head is resting on my crossed arms. My hair and eyebrows are black and thick, my eyes are almond-shaped and yellow, my skin is a golden-brown. There are more drawings and pictures of me too; and there are memories of being painted. When I was five, I sat in a big green chair so that my dad could paint me in oils, and I fidgeted and pulled as many faces as possible while my dad frustratedly tried to capture a still version of me.

My dad now makes sculptures out of household dust; but, when I was very young, he was primarily a painter. And, by depicting me in his preferred medium, he was, in a sense, letting me into his life – into all aspects of his life, including his practice. There are similar portraits of children by their parents, in which child-rearing and art complement one another. In 1929, after the birth of her son Paul, the sculptor Barbara Hepworth carved a baby from dark Burmese wood, and she wrote, 'my son Paul was born, and, with him in his cot, or on a rug at my feet, my carving developed and strengthened'. Half a century earlier, the impressionist painter Berthe Morisot gave birth to her daughter Julie, who similarly became her muse; using the same colours with which she had previously depicted women sharing tea and arranging flowers, Morisot documents Julie growing up. Paul Gauguin created portraits in oils of his favourite child, Aline, who was born in 1877; after the birth of Henry Moore's daughter Mary in 1946, children began to appear in his work – in Moore's bronze sculpture, *Family Group* (1949), for instance, two parents are depicted carrying an infant between them; in 2011, Henry Taylor painted his son Noah, in his signature rough acrylic strokes against a mottled green background; and Cyrus, Shirin Neshat's son, born in 1990, is often photographed surrounded by the black of the artist's chador; in *Bonding* (1995), Cyrus's small hands are held in Neshat's that are overlaid with the Persian calligraphy she covers bare skin with in many of her works.

My nan's portrait of me was painted in her favourite medium, acrylics. She used the same set of paints that she had worked with over the previous few months to paint carefully arranged flowers in vases, robins, pastoral scenes and roses. I recognised this for what it was – a form of acceptance, a kind of welcoming into my nan's life. With all her favourite tools and her favourite paints, I understood that she had, for hours and hours – amounting probably to a few days in total – built me up on the canvas bit by bit, looking back and forth from photo to painting, her mind occupied, for all that time, by me.

In part, this was why my brain froze when I saw the portrait for the first time. My nan had never made any effort to get to know me; we had barely touched throughout my childhood – only a small area of our cheeks had brushed one another when we formally kissed each other goodbye after each visit; for a long time the only things she said to me were that no man would ever fall in love with me because I bit my nails; that I was thin but that I'd get fat like her soon; and, in a disappointed voice, that I didn't wear dresses often. When my cousins once visited my nan and granddad at the same time as me and my parents, they received little bags of sweets and chocolates, while I sat and watched empty-handed from a corner of the room that felt like it existed in a completely separate dimension. I never felt a part of the family, and this magnified my feeling of being different and an outsider in my day-to-day life in the majority white town we lived in. Growing up, I felt like I had no real English family – only a fake family that I pretended to be related to. Other than my dad, none of them talked to me as if I was related to them. I wondered whether – with their aversion to most things foreign – perhaps they simply couldn't relate to me as family.

So why has she painted me? I wondered. My nan, as far as I could tell, didn't love me; and there was no other sign apart from the painting itself – which depicted, it seemed, only my English half – that she was accepting me into her life. I considered whether, perhaps, she was trying to actively erase the Japanese side of me, so that she could begin to accept me; my grandparents had grown up during the Second World War and I knew that, during that time, Japanese people were represented as only an uncivilised enemy. I knew also that when I was little, my nan had questioned my mum about why she was teaching me Japanese, when we were living in

England. Quite quickly, though, I moved on; I forgot about the painting completely and life continued as it always had.

Only recently, now an adult, have I started thinking about my nan's portrait again. I've told a couple of friends about my memory of it and, each time, they've responded with horror and shock, which is I think the right reaction. But, when I think about it myself, I feel warmth; and perhaps even love.

This isn't to say that the portrait itself isn't problematic. As a teenager, I'd hated everything Asian. I'd seen Asians mocked and dehumanised in film and TV and my mum's accent mimicked incessantly and inaccurately by English people; in the playground, I learnt that Asians had funny slit eyes; in the street and on the internet that Asian women were highly sexualised and objectified; that they were so weird and alien that even their bodies were rumoured to be fundamentally different to other humans' (they were believed by some to have 'sideways vaginas'); I learnt that messages left over from wartime propaganda still persisted too, and that the Japanese were seen by some to be a barbaric race; and then there was the fact that when I did well at school and at the violin it wasn't because I was intelligent or gifted, but because I was Asian, or because my mum was a 'tiger mum' (which, in reality, she wasn't at all).

I spent many years not wanting to be Asian; I believed Asians couldn't be good-looking, characterful, independent or creative (my mum was an exception to this as I'd heard her white friends say things like 'you're nothing like a

Japanese woman!' thinking it was a compliment), and that I could only be these things myself because of my white half. I pushed my Japanese half away to the extent that, when my Japanese granddad visited, I made no attempt to get to know him. A portrait painted by a family member, with the Asian half of me erased, validated my behaviour and my beliefs.

However, my nan did not paint my portrait with this as her intention. A painting, I think, is always a labour of love. Sometime between 600 and 700 BCE, a shepherdess called Kora of Sicyon positioned her lover, who was due to leave on a long journey the next day, in front of a light source and she marked on the wall the outline of his shadow so that she wouldn't forget him. Kora's father, Butades, filled the outline with red clay and fired the clay in a kiln to preserve the image of his daughter's lover for her. For a long time, this has been falsely credited with being the origin story of painting (while, in fact, it is the origin story of bas-relief sculpture); poets have written about Kora's outline as being the first painting, and artists have reimagined her tracing around her lover's shadow in their own works, for centuries, with titles including *The Origin of Painting* (1786, Jean Baptiste Regnault; 1795, Benjamin West; 1830, Karl Friedrich Schinkel; 1831, Heinrich Eddelien) and *The Origin of Drawing* (1829, Anne-Louis Girodet-Trioson; 1984, Dianne Blell; 2008, Antony Gormley). In his *Essay on the Origin of Languages* Jean-Jacques Rousseau wrote that 'Love, it is said, was the inventor of drawing'.

The idea that Kora invented painting has persisted because the story of her and her departing lover neatly describes what painting so often is – an act of not only love but, also, preservation. In a similar vein, Frida Kahlo once explained to the artist Josep Bartolí, 'I paint flowers so they will not die'.

My nan has painted only a small number of pieces. Everything she has depicted has been something she loves – the birds that used to visit her garden, her dogs, flowers. It's notable that, of all the members of our family, she chose to paint me.

I realised years after the day we visited my grandparents that when we paint or draw portraits of other people, we almost always put something of ourselves into how we depict our subject. Basil Hallward, the painter of Dorian Gray's portrait, famously says in Oscar Wilde's novel: 'every portrait that is painted with feeling is a portrait of the artist, not of the sitter. The sitter is merely the accident, the occasion. It is not he who is revealed by the painter; it is rather the painter who, on the coloured canvas, reveals himself'.

What does my nan's portrait of me reveal about her? Now I am an adult, I recognise that it wasn't simply a way of omitting the part of me she couldn't relate, or even had an aversion, to. I wonder if it was, perhaps, in fact the opposite. She may have painted me to feel closer to me, and to understand me – the child who looked so different to her and yet came from her. She likely didn't deliberately paint me as completely white, also; I think she only did what she knew how – to depict skin as she knew it, and hair as she knew it; to build a face using the colours she had been taught to use in her painting classes perhaps – whites, beiges, pinks; the same colours I was also taught to use to create 'skin colour' at school.

I've gradually got to know my nan a little better over the last few years. Throughout my childhood, there was nothing at all that connected me to her – I looked different to her, I liked different foods to her, I spoke sometimes in a different language to her. But, now, my nan and I have something in common; we are both women – and, when we talk on the phone, there is a familiarity that never existed before. During spring 2020, at the end of a phone call before hanging up, my nan said 'love you' – the first time she had ever mentioned anything about love to me; it didn't feel like a sudden revelation, or an accident. It felt like a simple fact that had existed for years but had never been revealed to me until now. Apart from once, when she quietly showed me the portrait she had made of me.

POSTSCRIPT

A month has passed since I wrote this essay. In that time, I've learnt from my parents that my nan admitted to deliberately whitening my skin in that portrait. She told my auntie – my dad's brother's wife – that she had 'toned down' my skin colour, and my auntie told my mum. And that is all I know. I don't know why my nan did it. But, now I do know that she did it on purpose: that she erased my Japanese heritage on purpose. And, despite everything I wrote in this essay, despite recognising that perhaps, still, she did what she did out of love, I do feel angry. My nan has done so little with and for me in my life; we never got to know each other; she never made an effort to spend time with me; she never made an effort to talk to me; and yet she did one thing – she deliberately removed a part of my identity and heritage in a painting of me and felt so comfortable doing so that she discussed it with another relative. I want to believe that she didn't do it from a place of hate, but it was a type of violence, like a part of me was cut out by her, that her paintbrush was sharp as a knife, and that it removed something from me that I recognise now as being precious.

I wanted this essay to have a neat ending. I hoped to tie it up and end on a positive note, and for it to be healing. But, reality is complicated; my nan and her relationship with me is complicated; race is complicated.

The Deafening Silence of Divorce

Amy Poon

I don't remember telling my parents I was getting divorced. I have no memory of an awkward conversation, or indeed a conversation at all, but that's probably because there wasn't one. You see, divorce is not a topic that can be easily disguised or translated into food language – the only language that most Chinese people I know are able to communicate in. 'Did you eat? Are you full yet? Drink your soup! Have some more! I saved you a drumstick . . .' These are all ways of asking how you are and expressing concern and love. As a caveat, I would say, of course, that mine is not a typical Chinese family – whatever that is. My father was always the black sheep amongst his siblings – far too gregarious, extravagant, petulant, generous, extroverted – in thought, word and deed. We, my parents and I, are unusually tactile, we kiss and hug and hold hands, link arms and snuggle a lot. We look close. So, it is perhaps surprising that even we did not manage a conversation, let alone a meaningful one, about one of life's most stressful and traumatic events.

I speak 'foodish' perhaps better than any other language as our family culinary history runs deep. My father comes from a long line of chefs. Somewhere in the long distant past is a many-times great-grandfather who was chef to an emperor – but the emperor probably had thousands of chefs . . . My grandparents had a famous restaurant in Macau where my granny was renowned for her knife skills. There is an old family recipe for Chinese Wind-Dried Meats, which we still produce today.

Bill Poon, my father, started in the kitchen young. In Hong Kong, he trained with a Swiss *pâtissier* and in the mid-Sixties he came to England in pursuit of my mother. Together, they opened the first Poon's restaurant in 1973 in Lisle Street, Chinatown. Three years later they opened the iconic Poon's of Covent Garden at 41 King Street (now a Burberry store). The great and the good dined there – from Mick Jagger to Barbra Streisand. In 1980, my father was awarded a Michelin star, the first Chinese chef to be given this recognition. Restaurants in Geneva and the City followed. Finally, in 2006, my parents retired.

Somewhere in all this, I was born and raised a Third-Culture kid, between different cities and countries, different cultures and cuisines. Not surprisingly, food was my one constant. I lived in Geneva as a child and after graduating, moved to Tokyo, Sydney and Singapore before returning to London to resurrect the family business. I met my first husband in Tokyo, we got married when living in Singapore and our daughter, my eldest, was born there. My now husband and I were both married to other people when we met seventeen years ago. And this is when we had to bring up the subject of divorce. After many a trial by fire, we are now a blended family, with four children between us.

I remember dinner, a big dinner, with extended family; my father is one of five. It must have been my grandmother's birthday – perhaps her eighty-sixth – and I had flown back to London from Singapore to attend the celebration. I was miserable, not quite in a Sylvia Plath kind of way and certainly without the poetry, but I was miserable nonetheless. Desperately, heartbrokenly, gut-wrenchingly, debilitatingly, anorexically miserable in my marriage, or so I thought I felt at the time. In hindsight, maybe it was just exhaustion. What was worse, perhaps, was that I had fallen in love with someone else.

My mother knew something was wrong. It wasn't hard to notice as I had shrunk to a size zero. She and I sat in the bar of Poon's, my uncle's restaurant in Russell Square, far from the madding crowd, and I vomited out a score sheet of home goals, fouls, off-sides and free kicks. I was unhappily married, with a young child, and involved with another man who was also unhappily married with two children of his own. My mother's response to this predicament was the most unexpected thing. She listened without a word and said, without judgement and without suggestion, in the most compassionate manner, 'How painful for you all.' In that moment, the dynamic of our relationship shifted distinctly from that of mother–daughter to woman–woman, and I have wondered since if she was ever caught in a similar bind, emotionally at least. That was the most intimate and the only meaningful conversation I had with my family about leaving my first husband. All other references to my divorce were made in passing and certainly never to me.

It's odd because talking about divorce is not something I have ever shied away from. It wasn't, or isn't, for me a source of any shame or feeling of abject failure, so much so that I even wrote a book about it (*This Little Piggy Got Divorced* was an unexpected sequel to my first book, *This Little Piggy Went To Prada*, which sold 300,000 copies). What I found infinitely worse was telling my father years before that I was pregnant. I remember blushing almost to the roots of my hair as it was an admission that, beyond a shadow of a doubt and despite having had a number of boyfriends with whom I had co-habited, I had most definitely and undeniably had sex. We were too buttoned up, despite being a family that cuddled, to admit to being that primal.

Shortly after I moved back to London, and before my decree absolute had been granted, my brother came round one evening for a drink. He looked a little drained.

'Are you okay?' I asked.

He smiled wearily, 'Just fighting your battle . . .' The conversation that my parents weren't having with me was being had with him – precisely because he wasn't me. Too painful, or shameful, or just plain hard to face, I think.

'She can get divorced if she must but why does she have

to get involved with someone else?' was the burning, indignant, accusing question.

'She's an adult, Pa, she knows what she's doing . . .'

'So you think it's okay that she's seeing a married man?'

'He's separated, Pa.'

'Same thing – what does that even mean?'

I can see my father now, shaking his head in disappointment and disbelief, and no matter how much it was eating at him, he wouldn't talk to me about it, never once asking if I was all right or why or how it had come to this.

My mother's approach was entirely different. What she couldn't say to me in words, she said to me with food, which has long been her mode of communication. For the rest of my stay in London, after my granny's birthday, my mother sent me soup to the flat in which I was staying: traditional Chinese tonic soups with medicinal qualities – red dates to nourish my blood, bird's nest and snow fungus for my spleen, to improve my skin, foxglove root to alleviate stress, *lingzhi* for sleep, cordyceps for energy and ginseng – so much ginseng – for my heart.

'Ma, it isn't my heart that's broken,' I protested. 'It's my marriage . . .'

'Same thing,' she countered. 'Drink.'

At times, the reactions to my divorce were almost comical. Years after my divorce and after I had my second child, my father announced – again at the dinner table, before an entirely inappropriate audience, apropos of nothing – that

57

he preferred my first husband and that Mimi, my first-born, was his favourite. It was one of those jaw-dropping, stunned-silence, zero-filter moments. I can't attribute any motive to this. My father is difficult and petulant and outspoken but he isn't mean. I think it illustrated how much my divorce had been on his mind. Like wearing Spanx, all that wobble that you try to contain has to pop out somewhere. My eldest looked at me, my youngest, Artemis, was thankfully too young to comprehend, my teenage niece and nephews looked at each other then quickly down at their rice bowls, I looked at my mother and in retaliation, my mother blurted out, 'Well, I prefer her husband now and Artemis is my favourite!' I still had a piece of *pipah tofu* balanced on my chopsticks. For some bizarre reason, a scene from *The Sound of Music* came to mind, the one where Julie Andrews and Christopher Plummer finally get it together in the gazebo and sing 'Somewhere in my youth or childhood, I must have done something good,' except in my head, I was paraphrasing, 'I must have done something TERRIBLE,' and suddenly I burst out laughing. My brother rather humorously murmured, 'Well at least he likes one of your spouses. Mine doesn't even get a mention!'

Entertaining or embarrassing scenarios like this seemed to happen around family gatherings, which, with Chinese families, inevitably involved meals. It was at such a gathering that my granny first met my now husband. We were not married at the time but I had recently given birth to our daughter. My granny was in her nineties, hard of hearing (though I believe selectively), sharp as a razor at times and occasionally muddled but still terrifying. She was very much dependent on my aunt, who was her carer, to shout into her left ear. The unenviable job of introducing this strange man to Granny fell to my poor aunt, who was as unprepared as she was mortified by the situation.

'And who is this?' Granny barked in Chinese as she shook hands (she did not speak English). No one answered. My aunt looked at my father. My father lit his cigar, made a show of wafting away the smoke and stepped back. My poor beloved looked at me enquiringly. I raised an eyebrow, smiled and shrugged my shoulders.

'What did you say?' shouted Granny. 'I can't hear you!'

There was a flustered sort of mumbling. My aunt laughed awkwardly. I would have said something but there is a pecking order in Chinese families as to who should speak when, and with so many elders gathered, it was certainly not my turn.

'WHO?' demanded Granny. 'Speak up!'

Again, my aunt mumbled something and feigned a coughing fit. My uncle decided we should all sit down and ushered us towards the dinner table. Everyone was grinning inanely, shuffling awkwardly, looking up and looking down, looking at anything but each other, but Granny was having none of it.

'WHO IS THIS?' she bellowed, banging her cane emphatically on the ground. I think she was thoroughly enjoying herself. My mother came to the rescue as only

59

mothers can. She took Granny's arm, gestured for me to join them, and, holding her hand gently, explained that this strange man was my *pang yau*, my friend, that wonderfully euphemistic word that the Chinese use to describe all romantic relationships that are not formalised by marriage.

'Ah, your friend . . . Your special friend?' Granny asked. She patted the seat next to her. 'Sit here,' she commanded me.

'Yes, Granny. My special friend. He's Artemis' daddy,' I ventured.

Granny took up her china spoon and drank some soup. 'An improvement on the last one!' she said drily. 'Drink your soup. Not so much rice. Fat is not attractive.' Reaching for a piece of chicken with her chopsticks, she placed a drumstick in my bowl, a gesture imbued with meaning as Chinese people consider this to be the best cut of meat and often give it to children as a treat.

I watched a close relation battle her divorce demons with some resonance. She had plenty of good, sound, practical advice from a good, sound, practical lawyer and yet she struggled for years to extricate herself from an unhappy marriage, in part for fear of the familial backlash. All I had to offer was a paved road. As things stood, she was the model child. I had been the rebel. First of all, I married a *gwei-lo* – a foreigner (my Hong Kong-Chinese boyfriend would have been preferable), then I had an affair and continued a relationship with a married man, got divorced and had a child out of wedlock! Nothing she could do would be worse than that!

As it happened, her divorce was all a bit of an anti-climax. When my relation finally untied the knot, I had a sweet message from her mother thanking me for my support, saying it didn't matter and was 'nothing, no big deal'. Her father simply emailed her and said, 'Let bygones be bygones.'

What is this lack of emotional display? It surely cannot be the absence of emotion. Is it cultural? I'm not convinced. I don't know many families, be they Chinese, English, American, French or German, in which divorce has been openly discussed. Perhaps it's just wisdom or plain old-fashioned good manners – if you don't have anything nice to say, then don't say anything at all. Perhaps it was precisely because no one said anything that my ex-husband still plays golf occasionally with my father, that my mother sometimes calls him and sends food parcels, that he and I can go on school skiing holidays together with our daughter, that this Christmas past we had planned to sit down all together to break bread – my parents, my ex-husband, my brother and his family, my husband and my two daughters – and, odd as it may seem, we were all looking forward to it.

We can't unsay or unhear things, and things we say and hear have consequences. They can hurt and cause damage as much as heal and give joy. So maybe silence is golden. Maybe I should be grateful for the silence. My tastebuds understood that someone cared deeply, so maybe I didn't need to hear it, talk about it, dissect it, clumsily, awkwardly, unnaturally. What could anyone have possibly said anyway that would have made any difference in a matter that ultimately concerned only two people? Sometimes, you don't know what you want but only what you don't want, so what was left unsaid would actually have spoken volumes if only I had learnt to listen with something other than my ears.

Ladyboy

June Bellebono

It's September 2018, and I'm at a vegetarian restaurant in Little India, Singapore. Opposite me sits my cousin. It's been almost two decades since we last saw each other, and it's the first time I'm meeting his wife and kids. He enquires about my trip to Myanmar, where I'd just been, and where his mum and sister still live. As soon as I mention that I went to Taungbyone Pwe, a spirit festival attracting trans spirit mediums, his eyes widen, he can't contain his grin and his excitement is palpable. 'Was it full of ladyboys??' he asks me. I sense his hope that I'll join him in mocking them. I awkwardly smile and nod – he has no idea that he's speaking to one, and that's why I went to the festival in the first place.

It's strange how 'ladyboys' and transfeminine people are immediately associated with ridicule. Parents use us as the butt of the joke to kids, straight men will laugh about having sex with us, cisgender women will be most offended when believed to be trans. Something about the defiance of manhood and voluntarily taking up femininity – from a body that is not expected to – seems to trigger a particularly strong reaction, almost as if threatened by the possibilities that could open up if this was normalised.

Over the last few years I've found myself over-analysing my transness, whether for a commissioned article or during a drunken house party conversation. I've wondered what brought me to challenge the gendered behaviours and expressions expected of me, and how I've become the person I am instead today: vocally cherishing my femininity and identity. Reflecting on my childhood and teenage years, there was a discomfort with heterosexuality and manhood, but that didn't naturally translate into me being queer, or a girl. I only really came to a deeper realisation of my identity after losing my gay brother, and shortly after, I discovered the existence of, and started researching, queer and trans Southeast Asian identities. These two events don't have any direct correlation, but they unconsciously triggered a new beginning: one was a rude awakening of life's volatility that forced me to be authentic to myself, and the other showed me new understandings of what my body and identity could look and feel like, outside a Western paradigm. Exposure, knowledge and self-reflection helped connect the dots. Things in my life started to make sense.

Maybe this search for clarity is what brought the nineteen-year-old me to apply for a Southeast Asian studies degree in the first place. Unsure of what to do with my life, I knew I wasn't informed enough about Myanmar and had a slightly voyeuristic desire to learn more in the hope of doing some future saviour charity work. Even though I grew up with my mum, who is extremely proud of her Burmese heritage and educated me on our culture from a young age, I am mixed with a white Italian father. Also, I lived in a small town near Milan where I never learnt or spoke Burmese, hung around Burmese people nor knew much of Burmese history – and I'd hoped my studies would help rectify this.

While the experience of being taught your own heritage in an academic setting from primarily white professors was one of the weirdest things that's ever happened to me (and one that I've often struggled with), I'm incredibly grateful for the knowledge of queer Burmese history I gained in my degree. In my last year I read *Smile as They Bow* by Nu Nu Yi, the first Burmese novel to have ever been translated into English and tells the story of a renowned trans Burmese spirit medium, looking at her rough past, love life, career, friendships and gender identity. It pushed me to challenge whether manhood was something I actually identified with. A year later, I was travelling to Myanmar for the first time in ten years, with the intent of visiting Taungbyone Pwe.

Taungbyone is a village near Mandalay, in Myanmar, and, for one week each August, is the home to Taungbyone Pwe – the largest spirit (*Nat*) festival in the country. It hosts a large number of Nat Kadaws – mainly trans women and femme gay men spirit mediums, believed to be closer to the

65

spirits due to their gender identity. People give donations to them in exchange for blessings. The festival takes over the entire surrounding area: on the one-hour moped drive to Taungbyone, we passed many villages, which have massive sound systems and people dancing, in an attempt to fundraise, with attendees throwing money in the street hoping to receive good karma. Taungbyone itself is insanely busy and hectic, from aunties praying from Nat shrine to Nat shrine, to young men getting day drunk, to LGBTQ+ people reclaiming the space. The energy is one of both a party and a highly spiritual environment.

What immediately struck me was the contradiction of being in a country with a law that states that homosexuality is illegal, and doesn't recognise trans identities, and yet has a cultural space for Taungbyone Pwe – where queer and trans people feel liberated and are venerated. The homophobic law, in accordance with other colonised countries, was introduced by the British during their occupation – and it's refreshing to see anti-colonial aspects of Burmese LGBTQ+ history, such as Nat Kadaws, still thriving today, regardless. When I was in Myanmar, queer and trans people were very much public and visible – and whilst their opportunities may be limited, their existence was not hidden.

In Taungbyone, they were the centre of attention. Even just looking at the crowds, they were admiring, donating to, and respecting transfeminine people as they performed in a display I never thought I'd experience. I saw first-hand how Burmese transfeminine people held spiritual and societal power and it provoked an intensely visceral reaction within me. I was mesmerised – their hair was polished and beautifully adorned with sophisticated accessories, their make-up was bold, their outfits sparkled and flowed. Some of them passed as cisgender women, and some didn't, but I don't think that mattered – their feminine energy was palpable, and powerful. I was frozen and thought to myself 'this is it'.

I have always struggled with masculinity – the movements that appeared so natural to the men around me felt so forced in my body. Wearing menswear immediately made me stiff, sex felt dissociative, my voice and mannerisms were always rehearsed. I learnt at a young age that my femininity had to be controlled and subjugated for my safety and peace, and any display of it would be met with violence. And so, that's what I did. I repressed every ounce of it as I lived in a hyper-macho Italian society, and gave in to restriction and reservation.

Despite this, I had always been read as feminine, regardless of my sexuality or gender identity – and I believe that's also due to growing up as an Asian boy in a white environment. Timidity, cuteness, innocence and sensitivity were some of the qualities that were attributed to me, and often contributed to the emasculated idea of Asian men. Reflecting on it now, I value these qualities. I value the fact that, in my experience, my Burmese uncles would often embrace softness and intimacy; that Burmese male dancers are covered in gold and intricate headdresses; that the Burmese national dress is *longyis*, a type of wrap skirt. Burmese men in their very existence, regardless of sexuality or gender expression, already challenge the concept of Western masculinity. And I was exposed to this whenever I visited Myanmar as a child, and feared this different form of masculinity for years.

And I believe it was these years of fear and control that catalysed such deep-seated emotion as I witnessed transness in Myanmar – I knew I was non-binary, but I don't think I really knew how that manifested in me.

I've been told that transness is a new phenomenon and a farce. Transphobes believe we should be excluded from certain gendered spaces for their protection. The same people ridicule and other us. Finding out about the existence of indigenous Burmese trans identities challenged all notions of transness I'd been previously indoctrinated in. On top of that, the fact that Nat Kadaws, due to their gender defiance and femininity, are believed to be closer to spirits and able to offer blessings (or curses) is in complete opposition to the satire Western culture usually associates with transness.

What resonated even more was that, beyond the spiritual significance, Taungbyone was also a *fun* space. Nat Kadaws have a charismatic dynamic energy, and are incredible performers. During my visit, I saw fire eating and intricate choreographies with a variety of props. They downed rum bottles and inhaled cigarettes to reach a state of trance. People danced and laughed for hours. In a lot of ways, it resembled a queer night out.

Parties have long held a special place in queer liberation.

It's where many of us first leaned into our desires, it's where we've been able to stop self-censoring ourselves, it's where we've felt safe enough to experiment with our looks and expression. And conservatism has used that against us – queerness is associated with being shallow, trivial, profane. Partying is so far from the idea of depth, yet here I was witnessing unmatched spiritual energy.

It clicked that my femmeness was a gift – not in the way it was for Nat Kadaws, but it was my only path to some form of unadulterated joy. It carried meaning. The abundance I was taking in was what I had to channel.

It's now been over two years since that trip, and every day, I'm still discovering new depths to my gender, sexuality, politics and identity.

Holding Burmese heritage has always come with hardship – since I was a child I've been aware of the army's cruelty and the struggles the Burmese face in their livelihoods. For years and years, I've had to follow the news of violence they enacted, from the attacks towards monks during the Saffron Revolution in 2007, to the ethnic genocide of Rohingya people in the last four years. More recently, the army staged a coup, overthrowing the democratic government, and brought back a military dictatorship. I will never know, or understand, or carry, what it means to be Burmese and live through these historical moments, and the fear and pain that comes with it. However, Myanmar has and will always be so much more than its military. And counteracting the awareness of the violence my Burmese siblings are subjected to, comes a deep celebration of Burmese culture – and the metamorphic power it had in unlocking pieces of my identity I was oblivious to.

I think my initial connection with the Nat Kadaws has slightly worn off. Our experiences, contexts and lives are wildly different. I have never lived in Myanmar and, despite my heritage, will have a very superficial understanding of what life is like for a Burmese trans person. My view of it is through a colonial lens, and it's easy to romanticise, and even fetishise, their experiences. I'm also associating language with them that they might not identify with (queer, trans, LGBT+) – I'm limited in understanding their lives, and also in translating them. What is unlimited is the fluidity of my gender.

And this knowledge comes with danger. It's a terrifying time to be trans in the UK. We're constantly attacked by the media, our identities are invalidated, our rights aren't protected, our medical needs are not met. It seems like we have more visibility and maybe our opportunities have widened, but the violence we receive has also drastically increased. Leaving the house is a fearful experience on most days, I am constantly prepared to be verbally abused, or worse. Somehow, this is still better than living in fear of myself. Femininity no longer scares me. I am freed from emulating masculinity – and if I ever do, I know it's purely out of safety.

I have been on a journey to understand the needs of my

body – what I want it to look like, what I want to age like, what makes me feel euphoric, what makes me feel stiff. I know I walk the streets and, with one glance, people will form opinions. Some people may see a gay man. Some people may see a faggot. Some people may see a boy in a dress. Some people may see someone who's just started transitioning. Some people may see a fashionista. Some people may see a disgrace. Some people may see an Asian ladyboy.

'*Ladyboy*': while it is a colonial and derogatory term that has now unfortunately even pervaded Asian languages, is probably the most translatable concept the West may hold to Nat Kadaws. And it's a term I'm no longer afraid of. Before leaving the house one day, my mother told me I looked like one as I was staring at myself in the mirror. I looked at her and thanked her. She stopped for a second, and then smiled back.

When my cousin used the term at that dinner in Singapore, I flinched uncomfortably. I found myself adjusting my body language to ensure he didn't think of me as one. Today, I would own the term with pride.

I don't know what my body will look like in the years to come. I don't know how far I will mould it to reach my happiest form. Maybe not at all. I doubt my Burmese trans ancestors had access to oestrogen or testosterone blockers, but they were as much women as the trans girls who can afford all the surgeries in the world.

For now, I take solace in that. I take solace in knowing that I'm a lady, who's also a boy.

Getting into Character

Katie Leung

My first memory of primary school in Scotland was when I started Primary 2. My teacher, Mrs Love, was taking the register, and asked me how I should say my name. She said, 'is it Lee-young?' And I remember thinking – *Lee-young*, that sounds like a really cool surname. That sounds like a white person's name, or a surname that white people will be able to pronounce. I'm going to keep that. Since that moment, I'd been telling everyone that my name is pronounced 'Lee-young'. It's only recently – up until five years ago – that I've thought – what am I doing? What *was* I doing? and I've started saying: 'no, my name is *Leung*'. It's mad that at the age of six, I was already trying to please white people.

I was born in Dundee, but I grew up in several towns throughout Scotland. When I was three I was living in Ayr. Then, my mum and dad separated, and my father, little brother and I moved to Hong Kong. I started school there, and remember feeling like I didn't quite fit in. We were being taught English, and the teacher would ask me to demonstrate how to pronounce 'butterfly' to the class, while I struggled to write the word 'car' in Chinese.

After about a year, we moved to Hamilton, a small town outside of Glasgow in the central lowlands of Scotland. That's where I started Primary 2, and I was the new girl.

My dad came to Scotland when he was fourteen with my gran (*popo*) and his four other siblings because there were no opportunities in Hong Kong, where he had a very impoverished childhood. My gran would go out and sell fireworks illegally, and the two eldest sisters brought up the rest of the family while she worked. My dad recalls going to work with her when he was three or four years old – willingly walking for miles carrying fireworks because he would be guaranteed food to eat. There were days that were so rough the young ones would have to be left in the cot with barely enough food and no one to take care of them. Eventually, my gran saved enough money to fly them over, albeit separately, to Britain.

My gran was so strong. Really bitter. Full of resentment. I see her as very committed to her children, very committed as a mother. She wasn't educated, she didn't go to school, lived through such a deprived childhood and had to bring up five kids, so I think that was why she was obsessed with money. All her children have become really successful – entrepreneurs, restaurateurs; the importance of money has been drilled into them, because they didn't have any. Despite their achievements, she still seemed deeply unhappy, and I often think – if she was literate, if she could read, could she have escaped that feeling, whatever it was? I don't even think she had the words to articulate the dark thoughts and loneliness that consumed her. Until she passed away, she was just this bitter old lady who couldn't appreciate what she had, but then, there is so much complexity to it: coming to a new country, not knowing the language, not knowing what was going to happen. She must have been in a place of such desperation to have left her country and started up here with five children and no money. Is that courage, if you have no choice? If you don't have a choice, what do you call that?

Perhaps it was difficult for me to fit in at school because everyone had been there for a year already. When my mum and dad separated, it was my gran who brought me up. We spoke Hakka at home, and she took care of my brother and me during our primary school years, while my dad went to work.

I remember being in Primary 3 and having just come back from the Christmas holidays. The teacher was asking everyone to name one present that we had received and loved. That year, I had got this Monopoly board game. Monopoly Deluxe. I was so proud of this present but I didn't know how to pronounce the word 'deluxe'. In my head I thought – is it *Dulux* like the paint on the ads with the dogs? Or is it *De-Lux*? I couldn't decide. I started to get anxious as it was nearing my turn. Eventually, she got to me and I told the class I got a 'Monopoly Dulux'. The teacher corrected me, and I was devastated. It was just another example where I thought – oh God, I can't speak English properly. And it's nothing, really. It's nothing, and everything.

The thing that surprises me, looking back, is that I was in a relatively racially diverse class. I think there were two Pakistani kids, and two Chinese kids, both of whom lived on my street, which was a 20-second walk to school. After school, we would play with the Chinese kids – one of them, Louis, is still my mate to this day. Now, I realise – oh that's why we were mates, because we looked the same.

Louis had four brothers who were also brought up by their gran, because their mum and dad worked in their takeaway. Our front doors were open all the time and we would be riding on our bikes, picking flowers from front gardens and giving them to our neighbours, learning how to make out with our cuddly toys. We lived in a tight-knit neighbourhood where everybody knew each other.

I think I was always aware of our Chineseness, especially in primary school. My gran grew vegetables in the back garden, and she would fertilise them with our urine. She kept an ice cream bucket in the toilet to collect it, and I would think – fuck, if my white friends come to my house, they are going to freak out. That's probably why I got on so well with Louis; his gran grew vegetables and fertilised them that way too. I suspect there was competition between them about who grew the best vegetables. So while the bucket in the bathroom seemed very shameful, having Louis experience the same thing made such a difference.

When my dad had a restaurant business in Ayr, his most popular dish was chargrilled steak, the whitest dish on the menu. White people would come specifically to have the steak. And then, in his restaurant in Hamilton, my brother and I would sit in the storage room and play video games after school, and my gran would be washing the dishes and going up to customers because she wanted to help out. It was hilarious seeing their faces as they wondered why this old Chinese lady was collecting their empty plates. She always felt the need to do something, she couldn't sit down and relax.

I helped out behind the bar when I was fifteen, just for some pocket money. After my dad broke away from restaurants, he would still visit those of his siblings. Every Friday night, we'd jump in the car and go to my auntie's restaurant. While the adults would hang out together, the cousins would have our own little group and help ourselves to the buffet, which was far more enjoyable than the authentic fresh food we were eating at home.

When you think of someone who hates school, you think of someone who played truant, didn't turn up, was a bully or was bullied, but I wasn't any of those things. I may have been a goody-two-shoes, but I hated school (apart from art class).

I'd spent two months at a secondary state school when my dad, who was doing well in his career at this point, asked my brother and me if we wanted to attend private school.

'Look,' he said, as he was driving the car one day, 'I wasn't educated, so I can't teach you guys. But the best I can do is make enough money to provide a good education for you.'

At the time, I was just surprised that my dad was being serious, because he's happy-go-lucky, such a joker. And I don't know why I made the decision to say yes to going. But I did.

Private school seemed very materialistic, but I guess it becomes that way, when you reach a certain age, and start caring about what you wear and what people think of you. It was like that ten times over at private school, where people were concerned about the latest iPod, designer wear and what cars your mum and dad dropped you off in.

Sometimes, I would find excuses not to be there. I had orthodontist appointments that were quite regular because I had braces and they'd need to be tightened. At some point, I'd fill in appointment cards to hand in to school, having mastered my dad and step-mum's signatures, and pretend I had appointments when I didn't. I'd leave for as long as I could get away with (as it was a five-minute walk from the school) and end up in the magazine aisle of Sainsbury's, browsing *Sugar* or *Mizz*.

I was always quite cynical about how the school fees were

being spent as I remember wondering why our uniforms – that were an added expense – were so extortionate while our textbooks were falling apart. Yes, I did the work, and my grades weren't bad, but I wasn't taught how to think for myself; I never learnt how to have an opinion – neither in school nor at home. Religious Education was the one class where we were asked for our views on topics such as capital punishment and abortion. I failed that class and I couldn't understand why at the time. Now I realise it was because, for once, I wasn't given a multiple-choice option.

Before *Harry Potter*, I had no prior acting experience. I'd been in a Christmas concert – *Bugsy Malone* – as a dancer, and done a poetry recital in Chinese school (when I got stage fright – to this day I can't do presentations of any kind), but that's about it. Although in primary school, one of the girls – a quiet, shy girl, 'the weirdo' – got the lead in *Joseph and the Amazing Technicolor Dreamcoat*. I sat in the audience thinking – I want to be 'the weirdo'. I want to be up there.

One day, I was doing my art homework in the dining room when my dad came in and said, 'Do you want to go to London on Saturday?' He told me there had been this casting call on the bulletin board after the news on the Chinese channel, looking for a sixteen-year-old Oriental girl. 'You're sixteen – you have long black hair,' Dad said. I was like: 'Okay, Dad, but I've never acted in my life'. 'Let's just go. I'm off work, you're not in school.' So I agreed.

On the day of the open audition for the part of Cho Chang, my mum, who was living in Brighton at the time, came to London too. My mum and dad hadn't seen each other for a long time. The enduring memory of that day was not actually the audition, which was not particularly eventful. There had been hordes of people still waiting after queueing for hours, and the casting team kindly told us they would just have to quicken the process and started taking in larger groups. When we eventually got into the building, Polaroids were taken of us in pairs. It was all over in five minutes.

It had been a cold day, and while we were queueing, my mum and dad went off together to buy me a coat. I was like – yeah, you guys, go and enjoy. Have fun! and they came back with this coat for me, which I still have to this day. For me, as a sixteen-year-old girl, the highlight was having this hope that my mum and dad were going to get back together again, even though at this point they were both remarried with more children.

After that, I got called back to London. There was a series of drama workshops and auditions at Pineapple Studios and people were being culled throughout that one day. By the end, I was in the final five.

I didn't have this urge or desire to be an actor. The more real it got, the more surreal it became. When I was in the last five, I was called in to do a screen test at Leavesden Studios, where they filmed the movies. There I was in the Gryffindor common room. The producers were all here. There was a camera. The director asked me to sing for the camera, and I froze. I didn't know what to sing. So he asked me to sing 'Twinkle, Twinkle, Little Star'. And then he asked me to spin around as I was singing it. It was all so awkward and new and terrifying. Afterwards, the casting director sat me in a little room and started saying things like: 'We're gonna have to take you out of school, but you'll be really well looked after. We'll have tutors for you . . .'

And I thought – I want to get away. I want to get away from school. This is a dream come true.

Nobody really prepared me for it.

In my first scene as Cho Chang in *The Goblet of Fire*, I'm coming down these stairs at Hogwarts after class. There's a brief exchange with Harry – we say hi.

There were loads of people in the production all around, just watching us. Who were all these people around me? I didn't know what they did. I didn't know their names. And the worst of it was, I was coming down the staircase and I could see this sea of people. I clammed up and internalised it all. I was just a nervous wreck. I was just like, *okay, just act normal. Act like this is fine, this is how movies are meant to be.* I now know the whole team are not there to judge your acting. They're looking at you for different reasons – lighting, costume, make-up. But I didn't know that when I was sixteen.

Once I turned eighteen, my mum didn't have to chaperone me any more. I loved being in London, having this independence. But even though I was a bit older than a few of the original cast members, I thought they were really smart, and they seemed to speak in a language that I didn't understand, with a level of confidence I could only dream of. They were talking about voting, elections, politics! I wasn't used to that – when I was at school, we were talking about boys, parties or dresses. In one of our breaks between filming, someone had the game Articulate, which I'd never played before. It came to my turn, and my mind went completely blank – it felt so traumatic. They seemed to be so much more knowledgeable than me. I started to wonder whether there was a difference between being a Scottish kid and a kid who was brought up in the city down south.

So I kind of retracted, I didn't feel comfortable socialising on set. I knew the conversations they were going to have were really intellectual ones and I was going to struggle with having an opinion on whatever they spoke about. So I found myself living up to the Asian stereotype of being painfully quiet and submissive and I hated myself for it.

My mum and dad are not your typical kind of Asian parents who needed me to become a doctor or a lawyer. But my mum was in finance when she worked in Hong Kong, and I remember looking at her and thinking – maybe that's what I should be aiming for – a profession that has more stability. I wanted to make them proud, and I didn't want them to see me out of work, especially because they had worked and were continuing to work so hard. So after the Harry

Potter franchise, I thought, maybe acting is not for me. I fell in love with photography and did a foundation year at the London College of Communication, and three years at Edinburgh College of Art.

I still had an agent, who would call me whenever the odd audition came through, and I went up for everything. I spent a lot of the *Harry Potter* money I had saved up on journeys round the country, often lasting four or five hours, for auditions that would never last longer than ten minutes. It was pretty brutal. And then the play *Wild Swans* came through, which re-set me on my acting journey, and I went to study drama at the Royal Conservatoire of Scotland in 2012.

So much has changed in the past couple of years as representation is more at the forefront of conversations now. Opportunities are getting slightly better. When I was at drama school, part of the curriculum included learning different accents. Once, I went up to the teacher and told her that I needed to learn how to do a Chinese accent, could anyone teach me? I thought I was being proactive; after all, I was going to need it for the roles I was going to get, right? The teacher immediately pointed me to someone in the music department whose 'natural accent was Chinese'. Looking back, I can't believe I did that, and put *myself* in a box. But it was because I knew that the *only* roles that would come up at that time would require a Chinese accent. Eventually, I would go on to fight for my character Lau Chen, in the television series *Strangers*, a headstrong, politically engaged activist, to have a British accent, although the original intention was for her to speak in a Chinese accent, something I refused to do.

I'm sure there were lots of roles I didn't get because of my ethnicity. It goes without saying that I was not considered unless race came into it. It's only recently that I've been in shows where my ethnicity doesn't matter. My first couple of jobs post-Potter were very specific.

Of course, I benefitted from the fact that when directors and storytellers thought of an Asian girl, it was *me* they thought of because they knew me as the character in Harry Potter. So imagine what it was like for people who didn't have the same exposure, but wanted to act.

I kept saying to myself – oh I should be grateful. I'm really lucky just to have a job. After all, I'm not going to bite the hand that feeds me. But then I realised that all these parts were really intense and explored deep psychological and political issues – the one-child policy or the condition of factory girls in China. While I was grateful that I played empowering female parts, I did wonder – can I also star in a light-hearted comedy? Why is it every time that we explore anything about Asia, it has to have these deep-rooted issues? Is that the West's only perception of Asia?

Within the Asian community, there's also a conversation now about the ethics of casting. Is it right for a Chinese actor to play someone who is Japanese? Or vice versa? Right now, there are not enough opportunities out there for actors to turn that kind of offer down. If there were, we wouldn't even have to consider the problem in the first place. That's privilege: not having all this extra stuff you have to think about.

For me, there is so much nostalgia attached with being in Hong Kong. It isn't just that I lived there when I was three, but I visited every summer as well, as my gran still had a flat in Tai Po in the New Territories. I love the smells, the heat, the humidity, the resilience and brashness of the people. They're not brash because they're rude. They're brash because they don't have a choice. Time is of the essence in Hong Kong and I've learnt to assert myself as a means to survive, albeit a different type of survival.

I went back to film the television series *Strangers* in 2017. The cast and crew practically took up this whole hotel in Causeway Bay. We took the tram to Lan Kwai Fong, to Wanchai and to tall towers like IFC. I wanted them to see the hustle and bustle; my mum was living there at the time and she would show us this cool food joint hidden on, say, the fourteenth floor of this unassuming building that looked like a dive. But, once you went in, it was filled with people, it was busy, it was steamy. I wanted my buddies to experience the atmosphere of Hong Kong. It's hard to pinpoint exactly what that is, as it's a combination of so many things. It's a bit like Glasgow in the sense that it's the people that really make Glasgow. The people make Hong Kong.

There was a clash of cultures. The Hong Kong crew worked alongside the British crew, and the miscommunication would sometimes be awful to see. The local crew were so efficient; they knew what they were doing, but from an outsider's perspective, it may have looked like chaos.

I was also disappointed with the way that Hong Kong was depicted in *Strangers*. I know it's a drama but Hong Kong is not this dark, moody place they made it out to be. When I used to watch cop dramas on the Chinese channel TVB as a kid, the contrast could not be more distinct. *Strangers* was just another kind of Western view of what Hong Kong is and it was so far from the truth for me.

It's very symbolic of what happens when people don't know Hong Kong, when they go for the first time, and find it too much. I'm very fortunate to be able to embrace both cultures, but it's also frustrating, because I am often stuck in the middle – wanting to get involved because I can empathise with both perspectives. To be honest, that's how I feel most of the time.

Ode to *Obaa-chan*

Naomi Shimada

My childhood growing up in Japan is distinctly infused with moments with my *obaa-chan*.[1] So much so that I can't separate thinking of Japan, the place of my birth, from her. When I close my eyes to try to remember her, to conjure her, to channel her into the room, all my senses, one by one, come alive.

I can feel her fingers lathering shampoo into my hair in the *ofuro*[2] while she gently, so very tenderly, leans my small, young, soft body back so I don't get soap in my eyes.

I can see her sitting across from me at her tiny table in an apartment that she no longer lives in because she got too old to live in it alone, eating one of my favourite dishes: oyakodon, udon, or yasai curry. I hear her reminding me to chew every bite one hundred times. She tells me I'm not allowed to waste a single grain of rice because for so much

1 *Obaa* is Japanese for grandmother while *chan* is added as a term of endearment. Like I would be Naomi-chan.
2 Japanese bath

of her life she 'had nothing'. But for me, someone who has been born into a life where I've never gone without anything I've really needed, I can't even begin to fathom that when she utters the words '*nanimo-nakattayo*' – *I had nothing* – she really *does* mean nothing.

I can feel her big soft ear lobes between my fingers. Always wearing the same gold studs my papa bought for her that time on a trip to Singapore. Out of all her features, I've loved her ears as far back as I can remember. She lets me play with them. I rub them because I think they are Buddha-like in nature and capable of magic. '*Ōkii mimi wa kikiyasui*' – *big ears are good for listening*, I can hear her say.

I am half asleep but I can hear her chanting at the *butsudan*[3] as the first rays of daylight start to enter. Her monotonous chanting of '*nam myōhō renge kyō*' floats into the last of my dreams and acts as a gentle alarm clock, a soft start to the day. I roll out of my futon where she was sleeping next to me and watch her so very curiously from behind the *shoji* door. The wafting delicate spiral clouds of incense and the grinding of her persimmon kaki wood *ojuzu* prayer beads all come together to create a temporary mystical land in the otherwise very ordinary living room. I

3 A Buddhist altar honouring Buddha, loved ones who have passed and ancestors that is found in most Japanese homes. In them are religious accessories, usually called *butsugu*, such as candlesticks, incense burners, bells, and platforms for placing offerings: such as fruit, tea or rice as well as photos, flowers, ashes and name placards of those who have passed.

want to sit with her, I want to know every detail about what she's doing: what does this spiritual practice mean to her? Who is she praying to? Who is she praying for? Does she believe in (a) God even though life has been cruel to her? Where does she go in her mind when she chants? What do those words coming out of her mouth mean? I'm embarrassed to ask. She's so transcendent. I want to be there with her – in this spiritual plane she's entering. I feel as though my presence is encroaching on the magic.

In many cultures, the act of love is not something we say in words or show with our bodies in the way of hugs and kisses, unlike how displays of love are thought of in 'the West'. In Japan, love tends to be more of an action, shown through acts of service, through cooking and feeding where love is tasted through every mouthful. Confusingly (and not without pain), as I've grown older, I've realised that love can also be displayed through criticism; love disguised as concern. I've taken 'The Five Love Languages Test' (a test that outlines the five general ways we express and experience love) a handful of times over the years, which always shows me the same result. That my main love languages are always equally split between touch and acts of service, a true child socialised in two worlds where love is displayed in nuanced and myriad ways. As far as I am aware, in Japanese, we don't even really have the language to say 'I love you' in the way it is used for family and non-romantic or platonic relationships. It's just not in the existing vocabulary. Love is displayed by showing up, in the simple act of just being there.

For the first chunk of my life *Obaa-chan* was always there. She was there for our births, our birthdays and after school. She grated apples for us when our stomachs hurt, dressed us in kimono for the holidays and told me ghost stories that still haunt my dreams to this day. She came on vacations abroad with us to places where she could not communicate but got by using her soft hand gestures, her kind eyes and us as her infant translators moving between worlds as if there were no distance between them. She loved being out in the world and the world loved her back. For so much of my childhood she was always there, until she wasn't.

I stopped seeing and speaking to *Obaa-chan* regularly when I was eleven years old. Our world as we knew it had fallen apart when my papa, *Obaa-chan*'s youngest child, her *musuko*, her baby, died from an aggressive lung cancer. It was caused by the asbestos that lined the railway standing above the vintage store, The Beatniks, that he had started in his youth. The store had previously belonged to my grandparents where they had sold Japanese tea, snacks and porcelain. My *ojiichan*, my grandfather, had died the same way before I was born. I am told they had both come home often coughing up black phlegm, for years. I am not told why that wasn't a big enough alarm call for them to change their lives. My papa was an enigma, with his insistence of doing his own thing in a still highly conservative Japan, his huge smile, walking around in his rare Hawaiian shirts and cowboy boots, his reggae band, his gospel record collection, his string of foreign lovers, his funny little *hafu*[4] babies, and his big, illustrious, complicated heart. To this day I love how he celebrated my mama for being exactly who she was – an enigma herself, a five foot ten, androgynous, strong-willed and strongly opinionated feminist Dutch woman with a buzz cut, at a time when Japan had barely any foreigners. And just like that, someone we all thought was larger than life was gone. He was only forty-one years old when he transcended this realm.

After his physical body passed away, a rift that had always existed between my father and his siblings morphed into a contentious chasm between them and my mother. Like after so many deaths when shock, grief and anger are masked as greed for money and other material remnants left behind. Things often left unsaid become internalised and explode, further hurting the already hurt, enacting even more damage. I will never know the ins and outs of the specific grievances between them all, but what I do know is these rifts seem to happen everywhere, petty heart-breaks have no borders. With *Obaa-chan*'s blessing, Mama eventually made a decision to leave Japan – a choice I understand better as I grow older. My mother was heart-broken, with three small children, in a foreign land where, even after being there for so many years, she felt alone. I know this because this is how she's always spoken about

4 *Hafu* – the most common Japanese term to describe children/ persons of half Japanese descent. I have debated this word in other pieces at length! Please search for them if curious!

it, and her experiences have involuntarily marked my memories.

And so the chasm became physical. On the cusp of the millennium we left behind all our friends, everything that was familiar to us, to try to press restart on our lives by moving to the most southern tip of Spain, a country where we knew no one. *Obaa-chan* was already in her eighties when we left. I can't remember how we said goodbye but I'm almost grateful for this lapse in memory. For understanding this reality would be too much to bear. It was as though multiple deaths had taken place, one physical and many symbolic for all of us.

Leaving meant we also stopped speaking Japanese, as Spanish and French words started to replace it. And so the mother tongue of my brother and sister that had once prevailed over their English disappeared in what felt like overnight. I, as the eldest, managed to retain some. I can talk about general things and mostly get by, my speaking level frozen in time, like the child I was when I left. Each new waking day brought new moments, brought new memories, but came at the danger of erasing what we could remember of the past. What price do we pay for forgetting?

In that time between us leaving and semi-adulthood, I don't really remember any communication between me and *Obaa-chan*. It was as if phone calls were too loaded. Phone calls made our absence from each other real. I don't know if this is a cultural thing but no Japanese person in my life reaches out. Just as love is displayed differently, the feeling and the act of 'missing' or thinking of the other is also not dealt with in the same ways. Calling someone up to say 'Hey I love you, I miss you,' feels like an entirely Western concept, I wouldn't even know how to say it in Japanese. Maybe it was just easier to pretend the other didn't exist, as maybe to acknowledge the existence of the other is to open up the door to missing them.

My visits have become more frequent over the last decade. I try to go back every year or every two years at most. I always have this fantasy idea of me and *Obaa-chan* catching up. I pack recording equipment, a Dictaphone, a handy cam, a plethora of film cameras, consumed by the need to capture the moment, just in case it's the last time, a desperate attempt to make up for the years we've lost. But the reality of my visits with her are instead beautifully humbling and I barely touch my ambitious documenting kit.

My *obaa-chan* is the size of a small child. When I hug her, it's because my Western, socialised self can't help myself. Her body tells me that she's not used to it but she doesn't mind. I try to explain my complicated life to her in the most simple way I can. I make shapes with my hands. She nods slowly but often and says many 'aaaaaaaaaa' and 'asssssssooos' – looking at me, her giant almost alien grand-daughter. She likes to point at all the *ōkii* (big) things about me. My height, my boobs, my feet. Everything about me is big compared to her. She has got much harder of hearing of late, so we don't speak as much. Still, I am frustrated

93

by my lack of capacity to express myself, ashamed that I don't have the words in Japanese to tell her what my heart yearns to say. She used to ask me about relationships, marriage, children. A few years ago, I was engaged to someone for a really short while. In that moment it was news I couldn't wait to share with her as every time I'd leave to say goodbye her last words to me would be '*Shinumae onegai kekkonshite kudasai Naomi-chan*' – *Naomi, please get married before I die.* That relationship fell apart fairly quickly and one of my first thoughts post-break-up was that I didn't want to tell her it didn't work out. I've been back to Japan a few times since and I assume someone in the family gave her the top line summary because she's never asked me what happened or what else is on the cards, and for this kind discretion I am grateful. So instead, we sit together, and we eat. We eat and we eat. She'll sit in silence till she notices something I've left on my plate, points and tells me I am to finish every bite.

Obaa-chan recently reached her 100th year around the sun. While writing this, I've also found out that she is currently unvaccinated against Covid-19, lying in a hospital bed, fighting pneumonia. Worryingly, the number of cases in Japan has jumped high enough for the country to declare a national state of emergency for the first time since the outbreak of the pandemic. After hearing this news, I cried because of the feeling of having no control over the situation, this feeling of helplessness, this feeling of smallness. As Papa is no longer with us, I carry what feels like a heavy burden of responsibility, as I know that if he were still here, he would be taking good care of her. I know I have to get ready for her impending passing, but after so much lost time, how can I surrender to this inevitability?

Obaa-chan I'm so sorry we left you.

I'm sorry I don't have the words to really say what I want to say to you.

I'm sorry I screamed at you that time when I came alone to Japan aged thirteen and you tried to get me to see my uncles and aunties.

I'm sorry about that summer I ran up those phone bills calling a stupid boy on his Spanish cell phone from your landline.

I'm sorry I haven't yet given birth to your great-grandchild.

I'm sorry about all those times I came back and spent more time hanging out with my friends than with you.

All I hope is that you know how much you live in my thoughts, how much I wish we'd had more time together, how much I deeply love and care for you.

I hope you think that I'm enough. I hope you see me as I am.

A couple of months ago, my aunt, who *Obaa-chan* lived with and was cared for by, suddenly passed away. She cried for her mother in the middle of the night and swiftly left this earth. Apparently my grandmother sat there crying for days. There are cruel truths to living a long life. You lose your children, people you love. You lose so many things. When I call, we speak for a few seconds. Calls that always end in '*Materu yooooo*' – *I'm waiting for you.* The borders are currently closed, travelling to Japan seems complicated for the foreseeable future, so as I plan, I pray that she can just hold on a little longer, '*Obaa-chan, mateeee ne, kuruuu yo!*' – *Obaa-chan wait for me okay? I'm coming . . .*

96

I walk, I run, I dance into the beyond

Anna Sulan Masing

In the space of London, I am aware of the private and public points of my identity. The public is where I create community, the private is more complicated. I connect with a general Asian-ness – or possibly diasporic – identity around aunties; I feel I belong when swapping auntie stories with friends: we all know aunties who tell you off for sunbathing because your skin will go dark, aunties who squeeze you and ask why you got so fat then make you eat two helpings of chicken curry. I also fit into an East Asian identity around food. The eating out in Malaysia that I did was predominantly connected with Chinese communities, therefore my public identity in the Global North feels more akin to East Asian-ness. I know my favourite dim sum dish (char siu buns), my favourite fried noodles (char kway teow), my favourite soup noodle (Sarawak laksa), and I can use chopsticks with rice (just). In New Zealand, where I partly grew up, and in London, where I live now, I could find home in spaces and people that are culturally rooted in Chinese heritage.

My private identity is one that has taken longer to understand and untangle. This is linked to a spiritual-ness,
non-binary approach to the world; a place where gender
isn't static, where gods visit humans and stories have power.
It is also a place deeply entrenched with colonialism and
missionaries; my history is one where my father was given
an English name at the age of eight, where land was divided
up by white men with big ships that had big guns. I got a
tattoo after I finished my PhD, which is (in Iban) 'my river,
my journey'. I am constantly mapping my personal identity
onto the physical spaces and world around me. Because of
this I've found solace and connections with the writing of
the identity theorist Karin Amimoto Ingersoll, who looks
at Hawaiian indigeneity through the connections with the
sea; and the Chicana writer, theorist and poet Gloria
Anzaldúa, whose journey to understanding identity is linked
to land – and to being Texan, Mexican, Indigenous and to
borders that shift:

> The land was Mexican once
>> was Indian always
>> and is.
>>> And will be again.
>>> – Gloria Anzaldúa *Towards a New Consciousness*

Of being indigenous, Andaldúa says: 'commonly held beliefs
of the white culture attack commonly held beliefs of the
Mexican culture, and both attack commonly held beliefs of

the indigenous culture [. . .] she learns to be an Indian in Mexican culture, to be Mexican from an Angle point of view.' For me, I learnt to be Asian in a white space (UK/New Zealand), and learnt to be indigenous in an Asian world (Malaysia). Whenever I untangle, weave and re-weave my sense of identity, I keep coming back to the concept of land. It is the soil beneath our feet, the soil that nourishes us, the soil that is toiled on and that seeps into my cultural history, through stories my grandmother told me, and the ones I now tell. I want to find other stories of home that rest in soil. But how do I be indigenous in my chosen home of London where indigenous narratives are not a known language, where connectivity to land is distant in the urban sprawl? How do we connect globally with the understanding of indigeneity? Where does one identity begin and the other one start?

My father is Iban, an indigenous people from Borneo. He is from 'up river', past Kapit, a small town in rural Sarawak, a state of Malaysia. My mother is a white New Zealander of predominantly Scottish heritage, from suburban Wellington. I was born in Canberra, Australia, I grew up in Kuching, Sarawak and Auckland, New Zealand. I have lived in London for over nineteen years, it is the longest I have been anywhere and it is without a doubt my home. My life has been about crossing borders, migrating, emigrating, moving, and staying put. Re-grounding has been the theme of my migration story – the reclaiming of space and re-creating of home, so that my mobility is not the same as being adrift.[1] Migrating is about meeting new audiences. I refuse to think of myself as in-between, but rather as encompassing all at once.

When I look in the mirror I sometimes see whiteness. I see my mother staring straight out at me in the line of my jaw. Sometimes all I see is black hair, heavy fringe with my father's eyes peering out from underneath; I see my Iban so clearly in my skin tone or in the way my body stands. Then, I catch myself reflected in a window and I see the whiteness in the way I lounge against a wall; nonchalant, hip propping up my torso.

And sometimes, I am completely Western when I inhabit my leather jacket and resting bitch face. Or when I don't understand the nuances of time and distance when travelling on a river through the jungle.

What I do find in every space I occupy is an awareness; I am aware of my mixed-race status and how that plays with privilege and choice – for and against me. Being mixed race, and/or coming from multiple spaces, but occupying a Western world is knowing where you fit and knowing how to fit in. When you look in the mirror you never simply see yourself, but you see the rest of society, who you are going to meet that day and what that means.

1 Explored in *Uprootings/Regroundings*, edited by Sara Ahmed et al in 2004, which looked to rethink the way migrant women are viewed, where there is stability in movement and mobility in being still.

From the *tanju*[2] I walk, I run, I dance into the beyond. I am an 'agent on the move'[3]; I have agency and dynamism *through* my movement and migration, and I want to re-see the journeys of migrants as such. Moving through spaces, places and picking up pieces of me as I go, creating pockets of home in every new location. But, in my privilege of being from nowhere and everywhere, I crisscross borders, get questioned but ultimately accepted, in painful contrast to others' journeys, whose identities are read clearly in the brushstrokes of their skin colour, in the accents of their English.

I am read as different but similar, holding a passport with cultural capital, an accent from a recognised place, an education in understanding border nuances.

Like Anzaldúa says ('as a *mestiza* I have no country, my homeland cast me out; yet all countries are mine because I am every woman's sister or potential lover'), I too have points in my identity that are recognisable and places I can belong to. I am open to construction for whichever world I am standing in. The UK border agent looks at my British passport and asks me why I was born in Australia, then tells me about a cousin who lives there. I then have to awkwardly explain I was only there for the first few weeks of my life and actually my accent is due to a childhood in

2 *Tanju* is the veranda that runs along an Iban longhouse, it is a public space for the community to gather.
3 Soda Ryoji's 2007 book *People on the Move: Rural-urban Interactions in Sarawak* looked at how the Ibans' approach to migration had agency deeply embedded in it.

New Zealand; they tell me how New Zealand reminds them of Wales. A group of Iban women in Kapit named all the features of my face that are Iban and proclaimed my Iban-ness, regardless of my lack of the language. I can stand and wait to be constructed and I can construct my identity to what works best for me in that particular space – to be different or to be recognisable.

Arriving in a new place means joining up with, somehow linking into, the collections of interwoven stories of what that place is made of.[4]

My journey to finding out about who I am was rooted in my PhD research. I went back to Sarawak, learning the Iban stories that women told in dance, poetry and weaving, and I found that space and place and moments were also crucial to this identity. I realised that farming was the link to everything. Food and the making and growing of food was the thread that tied so much together: the rhythms of farming, the myths of farming, the spirits and gods and souls of everything in the jungle. And so I learnt that I am from the jungle, no matter how far I am, the rituals and rhythms of the soil of the jungle sit within me.

Like my Iban forebears, I am a migrant who adapts to the environment; building, planting, nurturing and then moving on to begin again. Like my Iban cousins I am a migrant who calls more than one place home. My story becomes

4 This is an idea that Doreen Massey explores in her 2005 book *For Space*, where she looks at how space is a social dimension.

interwoven with each location, and each location becomes a part of my identity. I also bring past spaces into new locations. Memories and identities that were created and developed in previous situations get utilised in different ways and get expressed in new ways. These are intersections of my identity that are articulated for each new audience, and I have a choice in how they get presented.

Every time I get upset when someone decides to construct me to fit their need, for how they see my identity, I am reminded that I can use the language and knowledge of this Western world, to subvert or override that construction. Every time I have a choice to construct my identity, I am reminded of my privilege of choice, because I understand this Western space. My able-bodied, cisgendered, mixed-race, over-educated self is reminded, every time I am accepted into a space, of those able-bodied, white, cisgendered, educated points of identity.

When there is a reluctance to talk about race and identity I get angry because it belittles my constant awareness, the work I do around understanding how my identity is interpreted by others. I get angry because I work hard in finding a way to articulate my identity, my difference, so that it fits your understanding. And I get angry because by not seeing race you have stripped me of my heritage. If you don't see race, you don't see me.

I am sitting in my London flat on a wet Sunday evening in Hackney, rain hitting the windows, drinking wine and thinking of my ancestors breaking the land, pushing back the jungle for one cycle of rice and vegetables and all the best fruit. I am caressing the snake plant that sits on my desk, and dipping my fingers in its soil to check the water levels and thinking of all the houseplants that I have not only kept alive but encouraged to thrive, a modern miracle. I feel the soil and the rivers of Sarawak in me, as I read the stories and remember the heat of the sun and wetness of the air on my skin.

In Iban culture, farming is central; it starts wars, inspires migration, creates gods and stories. Where does a farming cycle begin? Is it with the harvest party – Gawai – where you celebrate the produce, bless the new planting to come in the knowledge that tomorrow is rest? Is resting the beginning of something new? Is it when the first shoots of the *padi* come through and you know the seed has taken to the soil and there will be a harvest this year?

Or, is it when you set out on the first day to the new plot of land, leaving early to beat the dawn, before the jungle wakes so that you don't hear the sound from any omen birds – in case you hear the wrong omen. And you go to the new hillside and prepare to break down the undergrowth, or to an old patch where that *padi* has grown well before and you hope it will again?

I am not a farmer. I am a Londoner, reading stories of Iban farmers in poetry, in myth, in fact and in research. As a migrant, as someone who inhabits multiple cultures I wonder which part of my story is important, which part of my private identity or public one can I enact and I wonder which connections I can lean into to develop kinship and belonging? For me it goes back to this idea of mapping space onto identity, for movement to be dynamic in its agency and about home and belonging. This is a concept that is rooted in Iban culture.

> In comparison with other Borneo peoples, the Iban are exceptionally mobile. There have been attempts to explain the Iban cultural preference to mobility. Freeman (1950) for example, emphasised that Iban need vast areas of land for rice growing. Their loose social structure and extensive kinship network allows communities to dissolve relatively easily and for members to join other cognitive groups.
> — Peter M. Kedit, *Iban Bejalai*

Moving is also a key factor to Iban farming and life. They use rotational farming habits as well as upping sticks and moving the longhouse to a new part of the river, or a different river entirely (hence wars, others are often there already). And they also just leave. The *bejalai* is a tradition (Kedit calls it an institution!) of leaving akin to a pilgrimage or coming of age that all – traditionally men – are encouraged to do; to be a wanderer, to show bravery in new worlds and to gain knowledge. It is important to note that a *bejalai* is about travelling, to come back again – to me this is important because it is not about leaving home, it is a constant relationship with 'home' and 'diaspora', and is occupying multiple spaces at once.

Iban believe there is a soul in everything, they are living within a rainforest ecology, sharing this space with the thousands of other living beings. 'Life to the Iban is a continual process of interaction between all beings, whether natural or supernatural,' explains Kedit.

I have chosen the idea that the start of the farming cycle is with celebration, the harvest festival. It is with a party, with food and drink and friends and family. A time full of stories, of imagining, of gods, of spirits; of ritual and ceremony where we are so close to nature that we breathe in the air and feel it pour out of our skins again. In this space we hold the past in our hands with the rice that we are eating that took a year to grow, the present in the company we keep and space we share, and the future as we think about rest tomorrow and that rest means the beginning of a new journey.

At the beginning of June each year, I sip on rice wine – tuak – from a bottle I have brought from my last trip back, my annual ritual of migrating this booze from one home to another, and strongly encourage my array of friends in London who I have invited over for lunch to drink with me. The sun shines, and the early summer warmth is comfort. I announce a toast and thrust my arm upwards to the heavens and the lukewarm, sticky drink tips out of my tumbler onto my fingers. 'To Gawai, to harvest, to beginnings!' I proclaim. I am holding multiple identities, multiple spaces, multiple histories in my hands at the same time.

Battle Ground

Romalyn Ante

'Nurses have always been in battle fields, even before Covid,' my mother says as she and I prepare lunch in the kitchen. She guts a defrosted bangus fish and blood spurts onto the white marble-effect sink.

It is April 2020. After working for five consecutive twelve-hour shifts in Wolverhampton, labouring from bed to bed, cannulating an almost collapsed vein, air-suctioning a choking patient, and squeezing steroid and antibiotic drops into a nebuliser chamber of someone whose increased short-ness of breath could collapse the ceiling, my mother is finally having a day off. The hospital where she is currently based has become even busier as the West Midlands has been declared a 'hot spot'. Tomorrow though, she will go to Wales to help another struggling trust.

When I think of Ma, I see a soldier who is missing an arm or a leg and yet inside, has an indestructible urge to run back to the war. After three glaucoma surgeries and with only one kidney left (she gave her other one to my brother four years ago), she is someone I cannot help but feel extremely concerned for. As a nurse myself, I know how this battle ground could rupture under the weight of a pandemic and suck Ma right into its darkness. I imagine my mother and our comrades – the nurses, carers, technicians, and doctors – scurrying like an army of pale-blue crabs across the mangrove sand in our hometown in the Philippines. The Philippines has a long history of nurses toiling through plagues, calamities and war as the Japanese occupation of the country occurred between 1942 and 1945 during World War II and propelled many Filipinos to train as nurses and auxiliaries.

I remember towards the end of the last *Habagat* monsoon of 2019, I went back to my country. I had been away for too long in England, a foreign home. As the plane descended, I looked down to hunt for the island in Manila Bay that forms the shape of a tadpole and thought about my grandfather's stories about the war that still live in me, especially the one about the Moonlight Nurse. I closed my eyes and heard not the propellers' hum but the ripples of the waters, the oars that sliced the waves. I could see a nurse in her canoe – without cover from the enemy's bullets, guided only by the misted light of the moon, quinine bottles clinking in her sack. Onwards – to a forest that sighed with guerrillas waiting for her footsteps. Nurse Carmen Lanot, a Filipina nurse in World War II, helped not only the local and allied-American soldiers but also the native revolutionaries. She forged documents to smuggle medicines to malaria-infested fighters. My guerrilla-grand-uncle, whose lips were gritted with dried blood and gunpowder, and his brothers would sing about this Moonlight Nurse braving a journey, and tending to jagged flaps of skin with edges that sizzled, even into her calmest dreams. Nurse Lanot, luminous in her white uniform, lighting up the makeshift wards by the woodland fishponds. I imagine her having the same composure as my mother. My mother who had the calmest smile, whenever she left our country for work abroad, or in the rare and stolen moments she took care of me whilst I was sick as a child.

Local nurses and aids who helped the American soldiers in the Philippines migrated to the US for greater opportunities, and hence, began the overseas journeys of Filipino nurses.

Now, the world relies heavily on migrant nurses like my mother and my colleagues. Despite this, an article published by the Manila-based social news network, Rappler, highlights the lack of nurses around the world: *A global shortfall of 5.9 million* according to the World Health Organization. Throughout the Covid-19 pandemic of 2020, the scarcity of nurses will be even more apparent: another article in the *New York Times* illustrates the fact that 'almost 16 per cent of nurses in the United States are immigrants, and nearly a third of those – the largest share – are Filipinos'. Similar to the US, Filipinos account for the biggest proportion of migrant nurses in the UK at 25 per cent according to the National Audit Office.

During the pandemic, article after article reveals that Filipinos have long been pulled towards wealthier countries for *higher-paying opportunities*. 'Higher-paying opportunities'; the words keep ringing in my ears. Beyond the idea of a gilded road, I see something else – the image of my mother drawing blood from the nook of my brother's elbow when he received dialysis treatment at the local hospital.

If we were living in the Philippines still, we would not be able to afford his dialysis treatment, I tell myself as I stare at my mother now as she continues to work by the sink.

That same treatment which, two decades ago, we could not afford, resulting in the death of my Nanay Lola, my mother's mother.

Ma now scrapes the fish with a knife, shreds of scales shoot across the countertop, briefly glinting in the slantwise sunlight.

'Nurses have always been in battle fields,' Ma says again, interrupting my thoughts.

This is Ma's world: an ambulance radios ahead, Ma and her colleagues know exactly what steps to take, as if their brains have been mechanically programmed for this specific crisis. They pull out a plastic pat-slide and raise it like armour as the emergency door erupts in a squadron of stretchers and a blitz of blue lights taints the immaculate floors. Ma and her team take one of the stretchers into the Resus, slide the unconscious patient from gurney to bed, as metal drawers clang open, followed by missiles of blood bottles and a salvo of needles. They flank the patient around his bed, catching grenades of dressing packs amongst the hiss of oxygen. One might throw a Guedel airway adjunct (a tube-like device for a patient's airway) to my mother. I picture my mother's hands (or perhaps they are mine, a few years ago, when I'd just qualified as a nurse) – lubricate the airway adjunct and insert it upside down so that the tip touches the patient's soft palate before it is rotated 180 degrees and advanced down the throat until the flange rests over the patient's lips.

My warrior-mother swaps with her comrade every two minutes to pump the heart of the unconscious man, her triceps burning for time and life.

'We have always been in battle grounds, day by day, shift after shift,' my mother repeats as she hooks out, with one finger, the gills of the bangus fish.

'Only when I stop, do I realise I am in a bombarded room,' she continues. I immediately think of dressing pack debris and medical wires tangling across the floor. Scissors and needles glint in bodily fluids and blood-soaked sheets.

Ma now salts the bangus, pats it with her palm as if lulling the already-dead fish to sleep.

Four months from now, in August 2020, there will be nationwide concerns regarding the lack of personal protective equipment as well as the disproportionate deaths of Filipino nurses and healthcare workers in the UK. The *Nursing Times* will report estimates of more than fifty deaths amongst the Filipino healthcare worker community in these mere months. The same article will highlight their interview with Howard Catton, the chief executive of the

International Council of Nurses, and the concern over whether the nurses were being asked to perform in 'higher risk environments': the areas I understand to be not just the wards that have been swarmed with Covid-positive patients, but other areas that have been transformed into Covid wards to provide for the surging numbers of patients.

A week from now, Ma will call me from the hospital in Wales, saying that she has observed that the PPE protocol 'depends on which ward you are in', which obviously means 'depending on the *availability* of PPE in that ward'.

A young Filipino nurse who just arrived in Wolverhampton two months ago will tell me, 'I am afraid to speak up when my manager allocates me to a Covid ward.' (These allocations were apparently part of their 'initiation training', which was different to what they had been told before the arrival of the virus). Nowadays they feel the management only 'throws' them to Covid areas. 'But I'd rather work and send money to my family. They need me,' she will say.

Twelve hours from now, my younger sister, who also works as an endoscopy nurse, will tell me about an emergency in which a colleague confused her with another Filipino staff member, relaying an important message to the wrong person. Instead of acknowledging this, keeping calm and carrying on (in that supposedly British way), my sister's colleague said, 'You all look the same!' My sister has been working within the Endoscopy department since she graduated in 2013. Seven years ago.

But before all these things happen, I am still here, with my mother, who prepares lunch for her family before she leaves for Wales.

Why is so very little known about our community? Especially when this country relies so heavily on us? These thoughts plague me every day.

Ma washes her hands and rubs them against her apron. The acapella of water on the sink quietens, the way my fellow Filipino nurses quieten like soldiers hunched in bunkers during bombardments.

Yet, I know too, that even though our voice may still be small, we choose which battle to fight. Which moments to give our attention to. Because in every battle, there are moments like these. Moments that do not require too much fire, but tenderness – those battles where my mother holds the hands of a patient who is chiselled with fear, after learning that the *query-left eye infection* has bulged into a tumour and swallowed a quarter of his head, or perhaps that moment where I find myself placing two pots of ice cream onto the table of a man who hasn't seen his wife and their newborn for weeks, and seal our secret with a fist-bump. Or perhaps, like that day when beads of sweat swell on my sister's forehead, as she and her colleagues stop whatever they are doing to listen to the carotid-tight cry of a son (over his deceased mother he is not allowed to see) resound down the corridor.

My mother carries the fish towards the stove. A vertical mirror on the wall captures her movement. She gazes at herself like a warrior reflecting in the brief, quiet breaths between battles.

'When you reach home, the mirror will only reveal your gunshot wounds,' my mother says, not particularly to me.

'Gunshot wounds?' I ask anyway.

'You know—' she replies with her usual soldier-composed smile, 'these blue, bulging varicose veins in my legs!'

We laugh as April light spills across the kitchen floor, and I realise how both joy and fear can congregate in laughter. We continue chattering, until my mother's words rattle the utensils and reverberate into splattering oil, sputtering salt, and the fish is soon fried.

Fluidity and Resistance – Ideas of Belonging in a Fractured World

Tash Aw

Not long after I first arrived in Britain as a university student, I interrupted two of my new-ish friends deep in conversation – talking about me as it happened. It was lunchtime, and as I slid my tray onto the refectory table, one of them said, 'Great, we were just talking about you, so now you're here, you can clear something up. *I* said you were Chinese, *she* is certain you're Malaysian. We have a bet on this. So, what *are* you?'

Listening to other people debate your origins in your presence is a disconcerting experience, but it's one that I've become accustomed to over nearly three decades of living in Europe. I've observed how these discussions have attempted to be more reflective, more self-interrogative, as people travel and read widely, and pride themselves upon being culturally engaged. A more typical discussion about my cultural identity these days tends to follow this pattern:

'This is Tash, he's Malaysian.'

'Um, I think you mean, he is *Malay*? That's the correct terminology, I think.'

This is before we progress to the tricky question of language.

'So I guess you speak Malaysian at home?'

'Actually the language is Malay. But no, I don't. I speak Chinese with my parents.'

'Oh, so you're Chinese? I thought you were Malaysian. I mean, Malay.'

Trying to explain being Chinese-Malaysian to anyone in Europe is a curiously dispiriting experience in which the simplicity of one's identity – which feels so clear and obvious – suddenly becomes tortuously complicated, a source of confusion and even, in these days of cultural sensitivity, a cause of anxiety. What if someone doesn't get it right? What if they mis-culture me? I can see the slight flicker of panic on a progressive white person's face when I say, 'No, actually I'm not *Malay*,' and they fear that they've offended me, that they 'haven't done their homework' – a genuinely awful dynamic that in turn makes me feel I should reassure them. 'Oh don't worry,' I say, 'I know it's complicated.' I lie through my teeth, because I don't think it's complicated at all. I am Malaysian by nationality, Chinese by ethnicity.

But what else can I say? We live in a world that is multi-layered, but wishes it were simplistic.

Nowadays I think of the condensation of my identity into either *Chinese* or *Malaysian* as a phenomenon that began with my departure from Malaysia and arrival in the West, at an age that marked my official entry into adulthood. In my mind, the transition took place somewhere over Kazakhstan, forty thousand feet in the air, as I travelled to attend university. The assurance of growing up in a country with an old, easy mix of races, cultures, religions and languages slowly dissipated, replaced at Heathrow by a system of categorisation in which I would often fail to recognise myself.

An easy mix of races and languages. I say this as a kind of protest and defence, almost by reflex, for I belong to that generation of Southeast Asians who grew up in the first wave of post-Independence, nationalistic fervour, and who had access to higher education, which engendered a natural anti-colonialism and celebration of local culture and history, with all its glorious messiness. We revel in the three-dimensional nature of our hybrid cultures and languages, rejoicing in the fact that we have an instinctive understanding of how the Southeast Asian archipelago weaves its cultural connections into a tapestry that remains elusive to most Westerners. *Such a beguiling mix.* This is what I sometimes find myself saying over lunch with some friends in Kuala Lumpur. We're all so mashed up! We look around the *kopitiam* table as we trot out these habitual phrases, noting the variety of friends present, some mixed-race, others in mixed-race relationships, all of us drawn from different ethnic and religious backgrounds. Foreigners – the *mat saleh, buleh, gweilo, lao wai* – they wouldn't understand this. It is our thing.

But the truth is that I have always understood what it means to be categorised. I also know too well the discrimination that such categorisation produces – that is the very reason for categorisation. Even for those of us at the table, the law in Malaysia is not applied equally. Some of us do not have the legal right to own more than half of their own company, or to possess certain kinds of prime real estate; do not have the constitutional right to become Head of State; do not have access to certain categories of government loans; have to obtain higher grades to get into university, and so on. Others at that same table have all those rights. The divisions are related to our ethnic and religious backgrounds (in rapid shorthand: those who belong to the majority group have privileges; those who don't, do not). It all comes down to the way we are categorised.

We are, at this particular lunch gathering, able to elude the uncomfortable question of what divides us by concentrating on what binds us. (We are now, despite varying social origins, middle-class, college-educated urban professionals, which helps this tendency towards smoothing over.) 'I'm not Chinese, or Chinese-Malaysian, or Malaysian-Chinese,' someone says – it's a line of reasoning I've heard quite literally thousands of times before, so I know what's coming – 'I'm *just* Malaysian. Isn't that so much easier?' The person who says this happens to belong to the 'wrong' category; she is a minority in a country that does not favour minorities. We celebrate our complexity by reducing it to a magical simplicity that in turn hides systemic inequality, because it is easier that way. I cannot help but notice how in Malaysia, as it is in every other country, those drawn from the minority or excluded groups are the ones who have to protest their belonging to a single country and culture; who condense and simplify their identity to the most convenient terms.

I'm not sure if we do it more to reassure ourselves, or those around us.

In 2016, seeking to shore up her fragile position as newly elected leader of the Tory party in a climate of post-referendum nationalistic frenzy, Theresa May said, 'If you believe you are a citizen of the world, you are a citizen of nowhere. *You don't understand what citizenship means.*' There was a further line of populist froth, attempting to equate so-called global citizens with hedge fund managers rather than with 'the people down the road', but by then I'd stopped listening.

There seemed to be a fundamental flaw in the logic of the first two sentences, as if they were totally disconnected. I couldn't see how one followed the other, how the first argument produced the conclusion – a classic *non sequitur* if ever there was one. Born in Taiwan to Malaysian parents, raised back in Malaysia from the ages of two to eighteen before moving to Britain to attend university, I had chosen, more than two decades ago, to make London my home. But, like every immigrant, I retained deep ties to my country of origin. My parents continue to live there, as do all my relatives and childhood friends; and the focus of my work requires me to spend long stretches of time in Asia, returning to my base in London.

By this reckoning, I am exactly the 'global citizen' May was referring to, yet there hasn't been a single week in the last thirty years that I have *not* grappled with the idea of citizenship. I am engaged in the perennial question of the meaning of citizenship not because I particularly want to be, or because I am tortured by issues of loyalty and belonging, but simply because I have no option. Travelling between London and Kuala Lumpur is a process of constant adjustment in which I am constantly forced to confront heritage and choice, the innate and the acquired, to understand how those elements compete for primacy in my consciousness at any given moment. Which is stronger, the identities – racial, cultural and class – imprinted upon me by birth and upbringing, or the ones I have chosen?

Linguistically and culturally, it is often a struggle, particularly in those liminal first moments, when the languages you have always assumed would be an indelible part of you take a while to return, and your fluency is stymied for a few minutes, hours, a day or two, and you think, maybe now I belong to that other place? The reverse is true, for example when someone picks you up on your pronunciation of a word in your more recently acquired language, and you feel like fleeing back to the safety of your childhood languages. It's simpler that way. Reject one place, retreat to the other.

Even from a purely administrative point of view, having

a culturally mixed background obliges you to think about the practical aspects of passports and residency permits. Why hold a passport from one country when you spend most of your time in another? And how much time constitutes 'most'? Fifty-one per cent? If so, what if you spend forty-nine per cent of your time 'away from home'? Or maybe it is tied to where you pay your taxes? But then what do we do with the ultra-wealthy who live permanently in London precisely because they *don't* have to pay taxes here? Perhaps we can evade tedious administrative issues and concentrate on our places of emotional residence, but that, too, contains an inherent illogicality: if I spend all my time in one country, whose nationality I possess, but spend every day wishing I lived in another place – because, say, my beloved, or my family, lives there – what does that say about my attachment to my 'home' country? All these attempts at categorisation are futile in producing any worthwhile conclusion on belonging and even loyalty.

I am far from being alone in my multi-sourced identity. I live in an east London terrace of low early-19th-century houses, the type of 'two-up, two-down' dock workers' cottages that were rebuilt by Tower Hamlets council in the early 1980s after remaining derelict for many years. Most of the street remains council-owned housing, with a large Bangladeshi population. Outside the houses, on the sunny side of the street, there are bountiful kitchen gardens grown in plastic and Styrofoam containers that produce chillies, tomatoes, beans, Asian gourds and bitter green leaves.

Sometimes large parcels of food and spices arrive from Sylhet, and I chat to my neighbours about their relatives in Bangladesh whom they haven't seen in many years. There's talk about applying for passports and visas, resident permits for young spouses, saving up for air tickets. The teenage children have never been to Bangladesh, and display an adolescent grumpiness at suggestions of giving up a month of their summer in order to visit relatives. Like me, they live in families divided by immigration, where questions of citizenship and belonging fill each waking moment, even when they are not articulated.

When I first arrived in Britain, one of the things that most fascinated me was the British interest in genealogy. At first I thought it was linked to class, a minefield into which I had blundered, and in which awe and resentment entwined with very British notions of the said and the unsaid. In my first term at university I found myself talking to a fellow student from an aristocratic family who expressed genuine surprise that people rarely knew the maiden names of their four great-grandmothers. It was less a statement of his feminist credentials – this was the early 1990s, after all – than a laying down of background credentials. In grand families, whose history was inextricably linked to that of the country's, even the women had names that you would recognise from your textbooks, if you were a diligent enough student of history. If you knew enough about your country.

But soon I realised that the interest in family origins wasn't just confined to the ruling classes. Almost every

British person I met at university had colourful stories relating to family origins – nothing fancy, maybe something turned up by their mother, or uncle or aunt who had done some digging in the local archives and found a nugget of information. (That was another thing: everyone had a relative who had taken on the mantle of family researcher.) My surname is actually a shortened version of the German original, because my great-great-grandmother married a Prussian soldier. My hair is this colour because my ancestors were Galician sailors who got blown off course and ended up as coal miners in Wales. My great-grandmother was a shepherdess in Cumbria. My great-great-great-grandfather was in the army in Corfu in 1800-something and absconded because he had an extramarital affair.

I'd visit friends' families, modest households that didn't boast coats of arms or ancestral portraits in the hallways, and would often find that one of the parents had painstakingly reconstructed their genealogy, the family tree meticulously traced on sheets of paper stuck together with Sellotape. Potted histories with a faintly nostalgic flavour would accompany some of the names, even when sadness was involved. Here's Great-Aunt Jane, she worked at the chemist's in Basingstoke where Uncle George did the bookkeeping. There's Cousin Harold, he died of tuberculosis when he was only fourteen, he was such a handsome lad.

On TV there seemed to be endless documentaries involving people going in search of their roots. *Who Do You Think You Are? My Family Secrets Revealed. The*

Secrets in My Family. Whether celebrities or regular people, everyone seemed to be at it in these programmes. What surprised me was how rarely the so-called foreign connections in these long-buried histories caused any major shift in perspective. The people who learnt that they were in some tiny way part-Spanish or part-Polish never saw the world with new eyes; they rarely, if ever, decided to relocate to Vienna to connect with their roots. I realised, then, that the point of such genealogical excavations was never to challenge the foundations of belonging, but to reinforce attachments to Britain. Foreign ancestors, generally from Europe, are assumed to have seamlessly assimilated into a vague Britishness (and more specifically an Englishness). What was clear to me was that all of these enquiries served to emphasise the link between a person, or a family – one unit of people – to one country. No matter where they came from, or how complex or messy their identities were due to historic or ancestral trauma, people's instinct to belong, and to declare loyalty, was ultimately stronger than the urge to celebrate their differences, as if to do so might be seen as threatening; and so, by and large, they concluded that they were *just* British now. Just as all my life, I have heard people around me – ethnically Chinese, Malay or Indian – declare that they are *just* Malaysian.

Those of us who come from immigrant backgrounds of all kinds will be all too familiar with the futility of trying to piece together a family tree. In my case, as with so many others' I knew growing up, personal histories are entangled with poverty, deprivation, a colonial past, conflicts linked to nation building. They are also linked to flight: to escape and aspiration, both of which conspire to forget history and rebuild it in a simpler, neater fashion, except that it produces a narrative that is incomplete. We left X country, we were poor, we arrived in Y country, we worked hard, now we are doctors. Yet the generations that inherit this story sense its deficiencies: what forms, exactly, did those sacrifices take? Why do we speak so many languages in this household? Why do we speak the local language with an accent? Why are my grandparents always distant, or crying, or suffering nervous breakdowns? These were the kind of questions I wanted to ask my parents as a child, but they recoiled at the merest hint of interrogation. They changed the subject, or told me that they didn't know, or, most commonly, simply said, 'what is there to know? All that is in the past.' Soon, I stopped probing myself, colluding in the burying of what made our story different, and messy, and contriving instead to strengthen the narrative whose foundations had been laid by my grandfathers, immigrants from China, and my parents, the children of immigrants. Like so many others, their drive to create a simplified identity prepares the young, born in the new country, to inhabit only one identity. Yet this is impossible. Everyone knows this, but no one will admit to it.

In my years of living and travelling across Britain and France, I've got used to meeting people my age and younger who live in the region – and sometimes the same village – in which they were born. They grew up in the same house their parents and grandparents grew up in, and if they leave to work in the nearest city in their twenties they drift back to their home region in due course to raise a family. I used to find it exotic, and vaguely enviable, to possess such a simple, uniform narrative about oneself and one's family, but I realised that I, too, was complicit in the homogenising of these backgrounds. I wanted them to be one-dimensional and tranquil because they offered a counterpoint to my own identity, which was more obviously messy. I remained blind to the schisms that these apparently flatline trajectories contained: tales of escape across class lines, educational barriers; people fleeing the pressures of being a woman in conservative rural Britain in the 1970s, or gay and transgender teenagers growing up in a remote village even today. A simple move across just one county boundary, say from Haslemere to London, might in some cases involve a switch in identities so complex that those people can no longer return to their 'hometown' for anything other than a fleeting visit. In their new lives they are likely to eat food that is totally different to that of their childhoods – *foreign food*, in short – and they will probably have the freedom to work as they wish (or not), dress as they want to and have sex with people of their choosing. Visits home might be strained and frustrated; their reinvention is so complete that they might as well have emigrated to Thailand.

I grew up in a time and country where escape was linked to a sense of shame – *our ancestors fled China because of the famine and civil war, they were starving* – which is hardwired into the notion of being an immigrant. Add to this the various forms of structural discrimination and it's clear why we seek to be *just* Malaysian, or *just* British, or *just* anything else. We want to be categorised in the easiest possible manner because we hope to elude discrimination – to escape shame. But in the world and era that I now inhabit, flight represents not only shame but empowerment. It might be born out of necessity – in general people *have* to move, because of safety, work, sexuality, and so on – but the lack of choice produces a greater set of choices, which in turn produces more complex layers of identity.

If the idea of imagined communities can explain nationalism by connecting easily identifiable impulses – cheering sports teams, pride at hearing the national anthem and so on – it must also be able to form communities based on more elusive commonalities, our shared differences, if you like. In this era of global fluidity, a refusal to condense our identities provides a comfort that simplifying them can no longer do. As we face greater pressures to identify with one clan – to declare loyalty and self-categorise in the narrowest possible terms – it feels more powerful to insist on the difficult pluralities of our existence than to deny them.

How To Name Yourself

Rowan Hisayo Buchanan

We look at the newly married couple. Their faces are round and happy. He's had a beer, meanwhile her lemonade rests by her hand. They're going to have a baby. She isn't showing, but we all glance at her stomach anyway. She touches it protectively. Then someone asks, *Have you thought of a name?*

She has a list on her phone and I scroll down. There are more names for girls than boys. She tells us she'd prefer a girl. The husband adds that it is harder to think of boys' names because he disliked most of his male classmates and by extension their names. The couple tell us that the names they like are — *English, unusual, but not too unusual, nothing weird, classic.*

I'm surprised at *English*. It sticks with me after we have gone our separate ways. I hadn't expected that criterion. They live in England and they are both Northern European in appearance. That the baby's name will be English is not a shock. What I'm startled by is their explicit desire to sew national loyalty into the name of this unborn child. But perhaps names are always a way of telling a baby who you want it to be and where you want it to belong.

Naming a baby is like trying to cast a spell. Do you want this baby to resemble its grandfather or your favourite singer? Do you hope the baby will be bold, brave, unique, serious, relaxed or ambitious?

Do you know what your parents wished for you?

Some things my parents wished for me to have:

A name that could be a man's so people might be less likely to discriminate against me.

A name that could not be shortened by bullies.

A name that all my relatives could pronounce – a tall order given that I had Chinese, Japanese, Scottish and English relatives.

In the end, they chose a name borrowed from a small red-berried tree. It grows across Europe and Asia. In Scotland, the tree is believed to keep away witches. The Japanese variety is called 七竈 and its name means *seven stove,* alluding to the fact that you can put it in the stove seven times and part of it may still remain unburned.

Once when I was young, I told my father that I wanted to be called Primrose. It sounded like the name of a girl who had ringlets and long eyelashes. Also, to me, it sounded like a real, English girl. You see, I too had once wanted to belong – because to fit in was to succeed. He said, *That's a cow's name.*

*

While writing my first book, I considered choosing a pen-name. Many writers have. Charlotte Brontë went by Currer Bell to hide her gender. The writer Ruth Ozeki goes by a pen-name for her literary and film work due to complications with using her father's surname within the wider family. Natsume Sōseki, a writer who was on the 1,000-yen note in Japan for over a decade, chose Sōseki because the characters mean 'stone gargler'. It is a name borrowed from a legend about a stubborn merchant. This merchant meant to say he wanted to gargle water, but accidentally said he wished to gargle stones. When his friend mocked him, instead of admitting his error, the merchant claimed the stone gargling was to clean his teeth. When I found this out, I laughed. It is a good name for a writer, a summoning of contrarian spirit.

I considered if I wanted to use my given name for my book. Buchanan is my father's name, one that his own father carried from his Scottish birthplace to the rolling hills of England via the Second World War. This is also the name of someone who, when his daughter anxiously suggested that she might want to be a writer, gave a deep sigh and said, *Okay but if you do it, go balls out.* I could have called myself 'Rowan Buchanan', but 'Rowan Buchanan' makes me picture a tall Scottish man with a deep confident voice, a man who kicks a ball around on the weekend, a man whose family are on the kirk records going back a hundred years. A good man, but a man who is not me.

So Rowan Hisayo Buchanan is written on each of my

books. Hisayo, my middle name, is built from two kanji: 久代. The first, 久, means story/eternal. The second, 代, means era/generation. It is a name full of wishes.

Someone at a party once told me they sometimes don't recommend books by writers with names they're unsure how to pronounce because they don't want to get them wrong. At readings and events, Hisayo sometimes causes my interviewer to hesitate. Before we perch on our stools at the front of the room, they take me aside and ask, *Can I check? How do you say . . .* They seem embarrassed and anxious. I'm sympathetic. But I want to hear my chosen name on people's lips.

This doesn't mean that I think it's easy. I am still ashamed that once I mispronounced the name of an Asian author I admire in public. I felt as though I had thrown something ugly in their face. I'd assumed an anglophone pronunciation. I wanted to write to them and say, *I'm sorry, I should have known better. I wanted to celebrate you and I have insulted you instead.*

I need to get the names of my colleagues right. A multitude of names and spellings in our bookcases means we're receiving a multitude of stories. Our shelves need more than Greens and Browns. And so we must all strive to open our mouths to new shapes.

I am proud of this writer-name. But now, I'm faced with a new choice.

Girls and women are often asked, *Will you change your name?* For me, the question had the loose fit of a hypothetical. That was until I told my friend I'd gotten engaged. Around us were the sounds of women talking and toddlers grizzling. At 11 a.m., mothers, writers, and mothers who were writers tended to dominate the café that we were in. I wondered which of these women slipped from one name to another. I realised I would have to choose. The name question returned over phone calls, in other cafés, on a friend's sofa. It came after *when?* and *how?*

My partner proposed by kneeling on the wet floor of a forest. The mud made two brown ovals on his jeans. I'm not sure why – aren't you supposed to get down on only one knee? I think that's what he did. But in the photograph I took, scared of losing the moment, I see debris on both knees as if, instead of proposing, he was praying.

I want to tell you that it was the happiest day of my life. I would be lying. The day *after* was one of the happiest days of my life. The day after, I rolled myself into the warmth and hope of the word *forever*.

But, on the day of the proposal I panicked. The ring was too big – it was vintage and cut to someone else's size. He'd thought we'd get it resized together. On the bus home from the wood, I couldn't stop spinning the ring around my finger. I was shaky. The waves of anxiety confused me. I was certain about this man. This man who remembered that I'd said if someone proposed I wanted it to be special but not public and not ostentatious and so had chosen a quiet glade in Highgate Wood on a rare clear winter's day. This man I love.

Perhaps that was the problem, the man-ness of him. He is not responsible for the history of women as chattels and still it loomed. Perhaps it was that I'm bisexual and I feared that people might see this as a straightening up, when it was only a falling in love.

Perhaps it was the Englishness. He'd once mentioned that a very elderly relative had expressed her wish that he marry a *nice English girl*, a person I am at only the greatest stretch. This phrase was worrying even though he assured me that neither he nor his immediate family cared. He is the first white English man I've ever been in a relationship with. At first, I feared his family would find me strange. I can eat an entire bag of persimmons in one sitting. They live in the Cotswolds and adore the Queen, rugby, cricket and National Trust properties. I wasn't sure how I fit. He pointed out that I too enjoy National Trust properties. Anyway, his family have always been gentle and welcoming and always kind to me. They have made space for my quirks. His mother cooks me lactose-free food and his sister knitted a copy of our dog. Should I take their name?

I placed my first name next to his last name on the edge of a notebook as girls do in movies. The person I saw was a stranger.

Once, long before the ring, I asked my partner if he would change his name for me. He told me his name had caused jokes and bullying when he was small, but it was his

family's name and he belonged to them. How could I dis-
agree? But, didn't he want to be my family too?

Names have potency. In 1587, a decree was passed in Japan
making it illegal for those without samurai heritage to bear
swords or have surnames. Many bent or broke this rule.
They wanted the status afforded by a second name.

The names of aristocratic and samurai-class women were
rarely recorded with clan names but when they were, it was
their father's not their husband's name that was entered.
Graves from the nineteenth century show the maiden name.
One possible reason for this, according to the UCLA professor
Herbert Plutschow, is that 'in the Samurai system, one always
belonged to one's own family, regardless of marriage.'[1]

Things changed during the Meiji restoration when, in
1875, it was ruled that everyone had to have a surname as
part of a system of family registries. My mother says her
family name Tanaka probably was assigned around then.
One of the most common names in all of Japan, it is drawn
in simple characters: 田中. The first is a rice paddy; the
second means middle. It's a name for people who farmed,
safely surrounded by others. When I was learning to write
basic kanji, I wondered if part of the appeal was the plain-
ness of the shapes. If you aren't confident with a brush,
these aren't too hard. I love this name. I loved it before I
could write it or knew its meaning, when it was only the

1 *Japan's Name Culture*, p. 186.

sounds that my mother told me were hers. I have wanted her name before I wanted to take any man's. I didn't reject my father's name, but I have always craved my mother's.

The battle about names continues. Today in Japan, it is illegal for a married man and woman to have different last names. It is more common for a wife to take her husband's name but the law allows a man to take his wife's. Because of complaints, concessions are being made. Some government agencies now allow women to use their premarital names at work. And as of December 2019, proposals to have passports display maiden and married names were being considered. (Previous rules state that under particular circumstances, a maiden name might be displayed but it would be in brackets.) Oddly, if my parents had got married in Japan, my mother could still keep her name. There is an exception for those married to foreigners. An acknowledgement, perhaps, of a splitting of allegiances.

I don't live in Japan. I am not subject to these rules. Still, I think of them. I think of how we rank allegiance, to country, to parent, to husband, to family, to field. A rose by any other name may smell as sweet, but in that story, children die because their names are different. A name declares who you belong to and I have often longed for a simple description of my origin. I have been asked in school corridors, pubs, Ubers, and graduate school drinks, *Where are you from?* and not known if they meant my face or my voice or something else altogether? I have heard people say, *You look just like your mother. Just like your father. Nothing like your mother. Not like your father.* People squint at my face and say, *Are you* . . . leaving me to fill in the blank.

A name would be a clue to strangers. I'm just not sure how much one word can do.

On a website alarmingly called success.com I read that you should choose a simple name in your job search, because people 'prefer Smith over Takamura because we're more at ease when we know how to pronounce something'. The website titles this section: 'Simple is Better'. And I think: better for who? Simple for who? But there are studies to back up such uncomfortable advice. A Swedish research team compared earnings between a group of immigrants who changed their names to 'Swedish-sounding or neutral names' with those of immigrants who retained their original names. The study found a 26 per cent earnings gap. Why am I surprised? I am descended from name-changers.

My grandmother's first name is Che-Chien. She grew up in Shanghai in a big house with a persimmon tree. She still remembers this tree and the sweet orange fruit. Her father was a factory owner with no sons and so he raised her to be a boy. In her childhood, she was excused from the feminine arts in favour of mathematics, science, languages. And though he later had a son, her education continued. She was sent to a Christian high school. She doesn't remember why – perhaps because of a dream of internationalism, perhaps because it was near her father's office. There, a

Southern Baptist teacher told Che-Chien that to learn English included being given an English name – Jeanette. My grandmother told me the teacher said it sounded like Che-Chien. This seemed ridiculous when I first heard the story. I've tried repeating one after the other and my mouth opened and closed to the same rhythm. It's a poor replacement but I can see the effort. My grandmother never liked the name. Later, fleeing revolution, she found herself moving to New York and she carried this English name with her. I don't know why she didn't change it. Perhaps losing a home and a family took too much out of her to imagine something she'd like to be called. For a long time, she would be bemused as to why she couldn't find a persimmon that tasted right in her New York grocery store.

Over the years, the name would morph to Jeanie, Jeanie-Liu and Jean. She never told the Americans her Chinese first name. She didn't want to hear them mangle it. As for her surname, she sometimes gave people her husband's Japanese name and sometimes her Chinese name, but in all that foreignness, no one noticed or cared. All of this is a common immigrant tale – but my favourite story is about the name she plucked from the sky.

As a young mother in Manhattan, my grandmother had no garden in which her child could play. They went to the park. The children gathered in sandpits and on slides and the mothers sat on benches watching. This being the Fifties, several smoked, nicotine trailing into the air. These women traded chit-chat. My grandmother found one divorcée's love life fascinating. But she did not trust these women – perhaps it was to do with their posture, or the way their eyes skimmed over her face, or their loud-voiced children. When they asked her name, she lied.

Mary, she said and smiled.

What I love about this most is the laziness of her choice. She named her daughter after a Roman goddess and an American movie star but she picked such a simple lie. For years, my mother would bump into these women in the street and be asked, *How's Mary?* And for a moment, she would think *who?* before replying, *Very well, thank you.*

My mother inherited some of this flexibility. In Britain, it is legal to call yourself whatever you like as long as you are not committing fraud. She could call herself Ms Teapot if that took her fancy. Instead, she sometimes goes by her last name and sometimes by my father's.

I could take my fiancé's name or not, and call myself what I like. But I want more.

'To pass' has multiple meanings. It can mean to walk on by or to travel through. My family have emigrated and made it onto boats and trains and been granted passports. We have been lucky. To pass means to be accepted to a school, to a society, to the world. To pass also means the process by which a person of mixed heritage may be seen as white only. Sometimes I do and sometimes I don't. I've received the surprised, *Oh, really!* And the squintingly curious, *Are you?* Or even the triumphant, *I thought there was something!*

I have wavy hair from my father and his pinched nose. The shape of my eyes comes from my mother, but she has double-lids – Asian eyes, yes, but not the ones the kids in the playground meant when they stretched their lids to the side. I have the roundness of my Chinese grandmother's face but something about the jaw line that makes my father think of my Scottish great-grandmother.

At times, I failed to fit in, to be accepted, to look or sound right. I remember being walked in on at the showers at school and the way my puberty-stretched body flinched. I remember the girls' sharp smiles and bright eyes and the way they commented on how dark my hair was against my skin – the way they pointed at my legs and armpits, the way each hair raised up on its own goosepimple, the cold air, and the shame. My mother has no leg hair. My father's sister is blonde. But there I was, too dark and too pale. Other failures to look right, to have the right memories, the right clothes, or just the fear of not belonging left me wrong-footed and awkward for years. At other times, I have passed tests I didn't want to. Men who told me their rankings of women by race. How they rated White and Asian and Half, and expected me to smile when they told me I'd done well.

I'm scared this is asking too much. But I don't want passing to be how I measure the success of my life. I want to build a place in which I belong and to choose a name I love.

When I decided I was never moving country again, I got a dog. Sometimes when she sees a new person, she stands on her hind legs, her paws hooked up in the air. They smile and bend and ask, *What's her name?*

Azuki, I say.

What? they ask.

Azuki, I repeat.

This name confuses people. First, because in British supermarkets, the word is spelled *Adzuki*. We spell her name the way we do because in the romaji system used to transliterate Japanese characters, 小豆 is written out as *Azuki*. Secondly, because many British people have never tasted or heard of these beans. But 小 means small and 豆 means bean. And she is my small bean.

The neighbourhood kids call her Suzuki. *Suzuki, Suzuki, Suzuki,* they shout when they see her. Her ears bounce up and down. I smile and wave.

One of my closest loves named themselves after a neon sign. They had been a toddler and young child in China, but they needed a new name after they moved to America. Their parents let them choose. Together, this family often drove past a business that would change your tyres and fix your car. The proprietor's name was set in lights. My friend grabbed that shining name to be their own. They held my hand when they told me that story. It is one of the stories they tell about themselves, grasping this new name for this new country. They are one of the best and bravest people I know, and they will officiate at our wedding because I cannot imagine a life without them in it.

Perhaps this was in my mind when I asked the man I will marry if we could build a new name together, a name for the marriage, a name for the home we are building together. Could we take some of his family, some of mine, could we stitch or knot them together? I looked into his hazel-grey eyes and asked, *Is it okay if it has some of my mother's name too? Would it be too much to take on my history?* He seemed anxious. He said her name and his name. He asked about work. He wondered what people would think of him. And finally, dear reader, he said yes. We have a plan but we haven't quite perfected the layout, hyphens, ordering etc. There's a lot to consider.

Being mixed race can feel niche. But I'm writing you this story, because maybe you're thinking about choosing a name for your child, for your love, for yourself. And you might be scared. You might be afraid that someone will judge you. Or it might feel too hard to tell people you want to be known as something else. I can't choose your name for you but I'll tell you I'm beginning with a list of wishes.

I wish this name will:

Describe a history.

Encompass two lives.

Spell the name of a home.

Be mixed and mixed up.

Be ours.

Vector of Disease

Zing Tsjeng

It started with looks.

Nothing serious, at first. A noticeable glance out of the corner of someone's eye; a discreet double take. A flick up towards the face and then the gaze hurled in the opposite direction just as quickly. Then people stood up, rather than sat next to me. Once, someone immediately vacated their seat as I slid into the one next to theirs. I could swing my legs wide, put my shopping in between my knees. A quarter of a train carriage to myself at rush hour – heaven.

I went to dinner at my Aunt Cindy's and my cousin told me about getting on the Tube with his twelve-year-old daughter. She'd coughed; people cleared the carriage. My niece wore the kind of expressionless shrug I knew very well. It was the same one I used every time I travelled on the Underground: *oh well, could be worse.*

I walked the five minutes to my local corner shop in a surgical mask my mother had posted from Singapore. A drunk guy came up to me, leering: 'What's on your T-shirt?'

Another man walked up to him; *my hero*, I thought. He simply pointed at my mask and then laughed to the drunk guy: 'No no no, corona!'

I felt myself grow hot and embarrassed underneath my mask. I went straight into the corner shop and stayed there until both men left the pavement and wandered off, clenching and unclenching my hands and staring at the freezer aisle.

Racism wasn't new to me, obviously. I still remember the blonde girl who threw a casual 'Alright, ching chong?' at me as I walked past her in Old Street. There were the men who bowed at me in bars; the ones who tried their luck cycling through every variation of 'hello' they knew in an Asian dialect (*'Ni hao? Annyeonghaseyo? Sawasdee?'*).

Then there were the other smaller, more intimate and hurtful acts. The men I'd dated who followed me with other Chinese women; the white friends who told me I wasn't 'like the other Asians at school', or the other white friends who surrounded themselves with Asians, gap year-ed in Asia and dated Asian men with an overfamiliarity that made my skin crawl.

Which is to say: I was already used to being sexualised, objectified or judged on my appearance; of being both desirably unique ('He's got an Asian fetish') and simultaneously totally replaceable ('His new girlfriend is Asian too!').

But coronavirus brought something different: I was feared.

I wasn't the only one experiencing this sudden shift in temperature. According to the Metropolitan Police, there was a 179 per cent increase in hate crimes towards East and

144

Southeast Asian people in London around the start of the first UK lockdown compared to the previous year.[1] In February 2020, a group of four men attacked and kicked a student from Singapore on Tottenham Court Road; one of them had shouted: 'I don't want your coronavirus in my country.' Three months later, someone on Twitter DMed me with the words:

> U R A CHINK
> U EAT DOG & CAT

But this disgust – though personally fresh to me – is nothing new. Chinese people have a long and depressing history of being thought of as infectious agents. During California's Gold Rush in the 1800s, politicians warned that Chinese sex workers threatened 'the health of white men'.[2] The Victorians believed that Chinese-run opium dens would ruin both the health and the morals of otherwise upstanding English gentlemen and women. 'What could all this grow to but the plague spreading and attacking our vitals?' wrote one Reverend George Piercy, a former missionary to Canton, of the growing taste for opium in 1883. 'It begins with the Chinese, but does not end with them!'[3]

1 *Evening Standard*, 'Race hate crime soared in London during Covid pandemic'.
2 May Jeong, 'Ah Toy, Pioneering Prostitute of Gold Rush California', *nybooks.com*
3 Barry Milligan, *Pleasures and Pains: Opium and the Orient in 19th-Century British Culture*, Charlottesville and London: University of Virginia Press, 2003, p. 83.

In the early twentieth century, white women who married Chinese men were judged by one British journalist to not only grow 'benumbed of all moral sense' but also to prematurely age, their physical features growing more 'Oriental' and 'befouled' by their intermarriages.[4] They weren't just penalised in the press – some of those who married Chinese men had to forfeit their British citizenship thanks to the 1914 Aliens Restriction Act, a piece of wartime legislation that aimed to catch out 'enemy aliens'. They even had to register with the police. In other words: *watch out! whatever these slant-eyed Orientals have – foreignness, disease, addiction – it's catching.*

These racist beliefs sometimes ended fatally. In 1900, Honolulu authorities decided to tackle an outbreak of the bubonic plague – most likely brought by rats and fleas on board a steam ship from China – with cleansing fire.[5] When it emerged that the first few victims were Chinese, prompting calls for the demolition of Asian neighbourhoods, the health board began setting fire to houses where people had died. The fire caught wind and destroyed Chinatown and beyond. Dozens were killed when five thousand homes – a fifth of Honolulu – went up in flames. The survivors of the blaze – mainly Chinese, Japanese and Native Hawaiian people – were driven into quarantine camps. When the plague came

4 Lucy Bland, *Modern Women on Trial: Sexual Transgression in the Age of the Flapper*, Manchester: Manchester University Press, 2018, p.72.
5 James C. Mohr, 'Lessons for the Coronavirus from the 1899 Honolulu Plague', blog.oup.com 2020.

to the neighbouring island of Maui that same year, its own Chinatown was immediately set on fire too.[6]

Other communities have also fallen victim to disease-related racism[7] – Jewish people were burned alive during the Black Death as the supposed masterminds of the epidemic, Irish immigrants to the US were demonised as carriers of cholera in the late nineteenth century, and in Los Angeles in 1924, Little Mexico was set on fire and bulldozed after an outbreak of plague.[8]

You would think that the advent of modern medicine would bury this kind of prejudice. But in March 2020, as coronavirus was declared a pandemic by the World Health Organization, US politicians – including the then-president Donald Trump – began calling the disease 'Wuhan coronavirus', 'Chinese coronavirus', 'the Chinese virus', 'Wuhan flu' and even 'kung flu'. The Chinese-American journalist Weijia Jiang drily noted: '[It] makes me wonder what they're calling it behind my back.'[9]

To some extent, I understand the temptation to blame things on external forces beyond your control. For Trump, it's easier to imagine yourself as the put-upon victim rather

6 James K. Ikeda, 'A Brief History of Bubonic Plague in Hawaii', scholarspace.manoa.hawaii.edu, 1985.
7 Stephen Mihm, 'The Ugly History of Blaming Ethnic Groups for Disease Outbreaks', japantimes.co.jp, 2020.
8 Hadley Meares, 'When the Plague Came to Los Angeles', la.curbed.com, 2020.
9 Carl Abbott, 'The Chinese Flu is Part of a Long History of Racializing Disease', bloomberg.com, 2020.

than the beneficiary of a collapsing healthcare system he inherited and perpetuated. It's often repeated that Chinese people in the UK are more prone to keeping a low profile and are simply allergic to attention-seeking. I'd argue that that is, in itself, a stereotype based on the cliché of the 'submissive, wilting Oriental'. It wasn't subservience that brought us out on the streets in 2019 in solidarity with the pro-democracy protesters in Hong Kong. It wasn't submissiveness that led a thousand Chinese people to march in London against racism during the 2001 foot-and-mouth outbreak – another viral eruption that was, at the time, blamed on Asians.[10] And it wasn't an aversion to attention-seeking that led us to set up the #StopESEAHate campaign in the UK, which has raised thousands of pounds for our communities.

Can people see through this patently transparent attempt to relocate the blame for the pandemic away from incompetent officials and onto a country that was hundreds of miles away, itself grappling with the death toll of a terrible disease? Maybe. I'm sure most of those who twitched away from me or glared at my mask would condemn Trump's words. Or perhaps I'm just giving them too much credit. What I'm trying to say is: I'm sure none of them think of themselves as 'bad people'. They probably don't think very much about Chinese people at all; we move through their

10 Stephanie Soh, 'In 2001, a British-Chinese Protest Against Virus-Related Racism', aljazeera.com, 2020.

lives as ciphers and symbols, stand-ins for the pick'n'mix issue of the day. That's what happens when you live in a country with minuscule representation, where there are more Jameses and Matts in government than there are Chinese people. You become something both more and less than human – you're not a person who happens to be Chinese; you're an *idea* of Chinese-ness.

Racism doesn't just exist in untruths and propaganda; it also simmers beneath the surface of the waking mind, prompting unconscious behaviour that sometimes barely even registers. The person who stands up as I sit down; the momentary distaste from a passenger as I board a bus wearing a mask. Call it part of the long-term health effects of being Chinese – the itch of moving through a world all too ready to see you as a vector of disease. Imperceptible to others, but as deeply registered as a rash under the skin.

After 'The Quinine Plant'

Will Harris

The more he thought

                              the more thinking
                              itself became
                              a source of anxiety
                              casting its green
                              shade over him
                              mid-sleep because
                              of what he was &
                              could not be
                              because of what
                              he did not know
                              he was

                              London he knew
                    it was the other country
                              in him he feared
                    the oak tree's unseen
                    roots whose tendrils
                    poked out mid-speech

did you inhale
diaspora
did you choose cliché
no
he said
not knowingly

The more he thought

                  the more things
                  came back to him
                  like the myth
of the great-great-grandmother
                  who left Fujian on
                  broken feet
                  sometime in the late
                  Qing dynasty
                  the myth of the living tree
                  divided
                  among her children
                  who became many
                  distinct seeds that
                  when cashed
                  became
                  one currency

The more he thought

the more he had to move
& soon he found himself
in Beijing expecting
the thud
of recognition
but as in a dream
he moved differently
walking the hutongs at night
shop after shop
different but the same
he licked
toffee apples & drank
bubble tea his feet
never touching
real earth

The more he thought

the more names appeared
Pekanbaru
Kota Bahru
Chiangmai
places whose names
meant something new
that was when
he remembered
'The Quinine Plant'
the poem he'd spent
years writing
then
one day
abandoned
he thought of the plant's
long waxy leaves
& white purplish flowers
cultivated
by the Dutch
as a vaccine for malaria
in the late 19th century
when his own Dutch
great-great-grandfather
worked at a quinine plant
in Bandung

The more he thought

the more he needed to return
to Peking University's
gated campus where aged five
he & his mum had lived
for ten months

a guard stopped him
at the gates & asked for ID
just as a man who
looked like a svelte
Santa Claus
appeared
he said he was a professor
of economics
he'd vouch for him

The more he thought

the less he knew
& sitting beside
the artificial lake
a part of him
remembered it
twenty-five years ago
snowed under
white as swan's down
the other part
connecting nothing
with nothing
& the sun set
behind
a plate of
green smog

The more he thought

the more he came back to
'The Quinine Plant' as a way to make
sense of his parents' relationship
as a kind of postcolonial romance
which made him its awkward
postscript

The more he thought

            the less he could extract
                some life-saving
            balm from the duress
                  of history
              without which
          what was the point
                of poetry

The more he thought

the less order took the form
of words to represent
the slaughter his family had
escaped the more
he thought of buckets
of fried chicken
his uncle brought back
from KFC where
he worked in Anaheim
in the late 90s
his cousin had
been there three
months and already
spoke perfect
American

he saw his uncle's
sweat stained
armpits
as he praised
Colonel Sanders

have more
biscuit
have more
gravy

The more he thought

the more he needed to purge
himself through walking
at night inhaling tree pollen
thrown into the air
by recent rain
so he walked until
his eyes were bleared until
he had to lie down
on wet grass
dreaming of the pages of
'The Quinine Plant'
buried in a green shade
& grown tall with
the blood of workers
a violent plant
which occasionally bore
small flowers
that smelt
of milk sweets
& made white people
salivate
though unfortunately
they were
poisonous

Mothers and Daughters

Catherine Cho

I remember that I used to trace a map of the world on the freckles of my mother's face. On Sunday afternoons, she would lie on the sofa with her arms outstretched. I would brush her hair and watch the sunlight from the windows flicker along the wall. And she would tell me stories about the past.

The stories my mother would tell me were fragments, with details that she'd continue sometimes years later. Her beloved childhood dog that was stolen, a boy who'd drowned in the sea, the teachers who would overlook her because of the holes in her shoes. She'd tell me about being hungry, about longing for a hardboiled egg, the memory of a red bean popsicle, of searching for sea urchins by the shore.

She knew I couldn't imagine this childhood, of hunger or want. I was her daughter, but I was an American, raised in Kentucky among fields of tobacco and corn. We spent our weekdays strolling along fluorescent supermarket aisles and Sunday evenings at Burger King.

And she knew that when I saw her, I saw only the elegant woman who wore sharply tailored coats and bright lipsticks, her past didn't seem to cast a shadow.

It was only on those Sunday afternoons that she let the edges of the past in.

As a child, I wanted desperately to know her. To me, she was like a celestial being – familiar, ever present, but unreachable. She was beautiful, with sharp cheekbones and dark hair with defiant waves.

Her love for my brother and me was fierce and overflowing. She seemed to betray no weakness – driving each day to the university for her graduate classes, coming home in the evenings to cook dinner while singing Korean love songs. We would hear her studying again after we went to bed.

She was comfortable in our hometown. She would let us eat frozen pizza on Fridays and signed us up for basketball when we begged to join the school league. She watched as we wrestled raspberry bushes in the summers and built forts out of leaves in the backyard. She knew how to shoot a rifle, to make coffee cake, to drive the sputtering Oldsmobile with the collapsing ceiling. But I wondered if she looked at the fields and miles of fence and thought of the ocean, if she thought of markets and tall buildings of metal. I wondered if she ever felt alone.

She never seemed to resent that I couldn't understand her childhood, and I imagined that there was a thread connecting us, tightly coiled, but one she let go of further and further.

Her English was flawless, and she approached language with a hard-earned precision. Still, she only spoke to me in Korean, language on her own terms. 'You wouldn't respect me if I didn't speak perfect English,' she said to me once, as though there were enough separation between us already. The accusation startled me, and I could only stammer in response.

I would think about this separation for many years, especially when I left home and I no longer spent Sunday afternoons by her side. I would think about the fragments of stories I knew, the ones I'd collected and constructed in some incorrect version of her life.

And so I was surprised, when my grandmother died a couple of years ago, that my mother told me she often wondered about her mother's life and everything that she didn't know.

My grandmother was born during the occupation in a country under Japanese rule. My grandfather was a city tailor, and they would marry quickly, before there were whispers about girls who disappeared, the unmarried ones who were taken to be comfort women, to be used by Japanese soldiers.

My grandmother would have seven children while working at the markets of a seaside city. And while the country was torn apart by war, she would have a baby strapped on her back while pregnant with another.

My grandfather was charming and a skilled tailor, but he drank, and money was scarce. And so his daughters would marry men who didn't drink – they had seen how weak a husband who drank could be.

I remember visiting my grandmother's apartment as a child, I remember we could hear the ocean. My grandmother would go to the markets in the early morning to buy fish that she would grill for lunch, and she would laugh triumphantly and show me the way they gleamed silver. She would cut trays of fruit and melon, the knife flashing in her hand.

I remember my mother would seem more like a girl – the way she laughed, the shine of her eyes. And I would look for her in the photos in their brass frames, a girl with defiant waves in her hair.

My grandmother would die alone in that apartment, and my mother would tell me, her voice shaking, that she wished she had spent more time with her. 'An ocean away,' she said. And it was unspoken, but I knew she was thinking of when it would be her time, and how she would be waiting for me, a daughter who lives across the sea, in an old world.

I live in London. To my mother, England is a place of the past, a place of shadows. And I know she wonders how I've stepped even further away from her, into a history that's not her own. I think of this sometimes, when I'm walking along the river, and I see the stones from the tides. I think of the ocean reaching for the wide sky, and I wish for home.

I imagine that I feel the pull of the thread, as she tries to draw me closer to her.

'I never thought I'd be without you,' she said to me

recently during a video call. And she looked at me strangely. And I knew that when she looked at me, she was thinking of a girl with an enamel clip in her hair and scraped knees.

Instead, I am the same age as she was on those Sunday afternoons, now with a son and daughter of my own.

I want to ask her if she remembers the stories she told me, but the ones she offered, I don't know if I remember them all.

The stories my mother tells now, are stories that I know – they are of my childhood, memories of my brother and me playing in the backyard, of Independence Day parades and Wednesday night church dinners. I know she will tell these to my son and daughter, and perhaps they will wonder if they know me.

And I will remember the edges of the past – of shadows and the light flickering through the windows, and I will remember tracing a map of the world. And I will think of her.

Bag For Life

Gemma Chan

'Take the rest of the noodles and the bak choy and you can have it for your lunch tomorrow.' My dad pushed the take-away containers and their remaining contents towards me across the table.

'I've got loads of food at mine, why don't you and Mum keep it?' I protested. I knew he'd insist I take the leftovers with me. This little routine would play out at the end of family dinners once I'd left home, and this time around, it felt both familiar and oddly comforting. Because it had been a while since our last dinner. Well . . . more than a while. The ongoing pandemic and most recent lockdown had meant that for months, like most families, we'd only seen one another through screens. This was the first time in a long while that we'd been able to get together for a meal. We were even legally allowed to hug (if we exercised 'care and common sense'!). I brought champagne to celebrate and we ordered from the local Chinese takeaway. I'd like to say it was a bid to support an Asian business that had been suffering, like many others, during the pandemic but – in truth – it was sheer laziness. We'd talked and gorged ourselves on crispy aromatic duck with pancakes, stir-fried king prawns with peppers in black bean sauce, and chow mein with beansprouts. My childhood favourites.

'Okay, I'll take them,' I said, 'but my bag's too small to carry the boxes.' My dad got up from the table and went to the hallway to retrieve his rucksack. He rummaged around inside for a moment and then pulled out a neatly folded plastic bag. He opened it out and offered it to me. I reached for it and then my hand paused in mid-air as I gawped in disbelief. 'How long have you had this?!' I asked, in genuine amazement. He shrugged. This was no ordinary plastic bag. Indeed, the bag was not of this millennium. It was vintage Marks & Spencer, made from thick white polythene emblazoned with *St Michael QUALITY FOODS* in blue lettering, the 'St Michael' logo in a distinctive handwritten style. If you shopped in M&S in the nineties you may well remember it. It's a classic. I've since found out that the St Michael brand was phased out in the year 2000, making this bag at least twenty years old. My dad isn't a man of many words but that night he'd had a few glasses of wine. He told us that he used the bag regularly, despite its pristine appearance, and that the last time he'd used it in the local M&S the cashier had shrieked 'Oh my lord, I haven't seen one of these in YEARS,' and made the other members of staff gather round to take a look. This moment perfectly encapsulated what I would describe as Dad's Golden Rule No. 1:

nothing goes to waste (which applies equally to food, clothes, household items, cars, everything really – things will be used until they break, if they can be mended they will be mended but rarely will anything be thrown away). This was established in his childhood out of necessity but even now, in relative comfort, he still treats everything with such care and hates wastefulness.

A couple of weeks later, I came across an article written by Dan Hancox in the *Guardian*. I had thought I was pretty familiar with the long history of anti-Asian racism and discrimination in the UK and elsewhere; the shifting stereotypes, the scapegoating, Yellow Peril and the like, and the erasure of the contributions of the 140,000 men of the Chinese Labour Corps who risked their lives carrying out essential work for the allies in the First World War. But this was a story I had never heard before.

In the aftermath of the Second World War, Britain forcefully deported hundreds of Chinese seamen who had served in the Merchant Navy during the war, deeming them an 'undesirable element' of British society. These men had helped keep the UK fed and fuelled via highly dangerous crossings of the Atlantic (around 3,500 vessels of the Merchant Navy were sunk by German U-boats, with the loss of 72,000 lives). Many of the surviving men had married and started families with British women in Liverpool – however, they were secretly rounded up without notice and shipped back to East Asia. Many of their wives never knew what happened to them, their children grew up believing they had been abandoned. The fact that this story is only just now coming to light, with no official acknowledgment or apology, might not be surprising but it is still heart-breaking and enraging. By the time I finished reading the article I was in tears and I realised that this had struck a deep chord, because my own father had served for years in the Merchant Navy before he settled in the UK.

My dad grew up as one of six kids in a poor, single-parent household in Hong Kong. He was the third child and the oldest son. My *ah-ma* (barely five feet tall, fierce AF, could out-haggle anyone) worked three jobs to support them. One job was as a seamstress, with long hours bent over a sewing machine in a sweatshop environment for less than the equivalent of £1 a day. Initially they lived in a shack on a hillside, with no running water. Then they moved into a block where they lived in one room, sharing a bathroom with thirty other families on the same floor. At one point they were made homeless after the block of flats burned down. After leaving school, my dad worked for years on ships – mostly oil tankers – at sea for months at a time, and sent money home to pay for his siblings' school fees. Only after they had all finished school could he save enough to pay for his own degree, coming to the UK to study engineering at Strathclyde University where he would meet my mum (her own family's tumultuous journey to the UK is a story for another time).

During my childhood, my dad was the most selfless and diligent father. His love for my sister and me was expressed not through words but through small acts of devotion: always cutting fresh fruit for us and making sure we drank two full glasses of milk each day so that our bones would grow strong, milk being a luxury they rarely had in Hong Kong; patiently teaching us how to swim (Golden Rule No. 2: learn how to swim). However, when I was younger, there were some things about him that I found hard to understand or bemusing: his obsession with education, his aversion to waste of any kind, his insistence that we finish every bit of food on our plates and him constantly reminding us not to take anything for granted. It was because he knew what it was like to have nothing.

After I sent him the article about the Chinese seamen, we had a long conversation on the phone. He doesn't often speak about his past, but we talked about his time in the Merchant Navy. Some things I remembered being told long ago – about how hard and lonely those years at sea were, how much he missed his family, and how dangerous it could sometimes be. On his third voyage his ship, a chemical tanker, was sailing between Taipei and Kobe when they were caught in the tail end of a typhoon. The Chief Officer went out on deck to help secure the cover of the anchor chain locker, which was filling up with water, and was killed when a large wave dashed him against the ship. He was buried at sea.

Other details were new. I found out that after seven continuous months at sea on his first voyage, he noticed that the white British officers and crew spent six months at sea at most, some serving four-month contracts before getting air tickets to fly home to be with their families. This was in contrast with the Chinese crew who usually had to serve long periods of nine months. Whilst some of his fellow junior engineers were apprehensive about being seen to be causing trouble, he represented other Chinese on board and took it up with the shipping company's superintendent. He found out that the British crew were employed under Article A (better pay, shorter sea time, paid study leave etc.), whereas the Chinese crew were employed under Article B (less pay, longer sea time, fewer benefits). The company told my dad he was the first person to complain. Dad told them he just wanted equal treatment and, as a result, he and the others who protested were allowed to fly back home with holiday pay. They had docked at Trinidad, so he flew from there to Toronto, on to Vancouver, then Honolulu, then Tokyo and finally, after three days of flying, he was reunited with his family in Hong Kong.

Hearing this story, it was impossible not to think again of the deported Chinese seamen, as one of the reasons they were considered 'undesirable' was because they had gone on strike to fight for an increase in their basic pay (originally less than half that of their British crew mates) and for the payment of the standard £10 a month 'war risk' bonus. It's a precarious business to simply stand up for your rights, especially if you are poor or a person of colour; and it unfortunately remains the case that those in power usually don't appreciate being held to account. I hope that one day there will be an official acknowledgment of this terrible act of state-sanctioned racism and of the wrong done to those men and their families. I hope that the surviving children get the answers and justice they deserve and that they can find peace.

The relationship between my dad and me hasn't always been easy – as is often the case, it's possible to derive both pain and gratitude from the same place – but I know how lucky we are to have him. And I will be forever thankful for the sacrifices he made for our family and for the things he taught me: the value of hard work, never to look down on those who have less, to stand up for others, and that a Bag for Life truly means life. I love you, Dad, thank you for everything. I hope I can always make you proud.

A (British-Chinese) Chef's Life

Andrew Wong

This is going to sound really strange, but the truth of the matter is that I never wanted to be a chef. In fact, when I was growing up, the main motivation for studying extra hard was so that I could avoid having to help my parents in their restaurant. Most chefs you hear about always talk about how cooking was their 'last resort', the vocational skill that saved them. I'm not going to lie to you all, I was pretty good at school, I was a straight 'A' student who went to read chemistry at the University of Oxford. I got thrown out, but let's not dwell on that.

I then went to the London School of Economics to study social anthropology and this time I actually graduated. People often ask me if studying chemistry and anthropology has inspired my cooking style. Again, now that I feel that we are all friends, I need to confess, the answer probably is 'NO'. I got thrown out of Oxford for having the worst class attendance record in their history and whilst at the LSE, I was there in person, but my mind definitely was not. In fact, the only thing I remember from the course was that everything always came back to one single question: 'is blood thicker than water; is what we do a product of our biology or our culture?'

So, how did I end up having one Chinese restaurant in London, one in India, and two Michelin stars? Well, whilst I was at college my father passed away suddenly from cancer. If ever you want to know the worst thing that's happened to me in hospitality, the day my father passed away, my mother and I still had to go to work and pretend to a restaurant full of customers that it was just another day.

Anyway, I was twenty-one, absolutely clueless but knowing that I had an obligation to help my mother look after the family restaurant. There came a long period of 'making shit up', pretending that I knew what I was doing when in fact I didn't have the slightest clue. However, between learning on the job and many sleepless nights googling all kinds of random topics such as 'can you fire someone because their breath smells?', we managed to keep the restaurant ticking over, ticking over, just enough to give my wife Nathalie and me one last chance to roll the dice, to go all in, to make one final punt on seeing if we could create a restaurant that initially was just 'somewhere that we would like to go to'.

I had a basic understanding of Chinese cooking at this point, I probably thought that I had knowledge of a lot more, but I knew that I needed to at least go back to China for some time to work in the regional kitchens to see if it was different. How different could they really be after all? It's just a wok and a fire right? So naturally, I did what any self-respecting twenty-something entrepreneur would do. I asked my mum for help.

'Mum! Can you call up all your friends in hospitality in China and ask them to let me work with them?'

She did and also requested that they ensured I ate three meals a day, that I washed my underwear and that I didn't go to any late-night karaoke bars, that this wasn't my gap year, and I didn't come back with dreadlocks and lots of dirty laundry. The best way I can describe my fake 'gap year' is by using the Cantonese words *'geen sick'* 見識 – individually the characters mean 'see' and 'know' but together it means 'life experience'. Although I was mainly in Hong Kong, I travelled hundreds of miles to kitchens in the north and southwest. So what did I actually learn amidst bribing chefs with cigarettes to give me recipes for their roasted suckling pig and Peking duck? I learnt about the sheer diversity of Chinese cuisine. After all, there are fourteen international borders and 1.6 billion people in China. Cooking is very different when you are in sub-zero Harbin compared to the chilli-addicted sub-tropical Sichuan.

One of the key dishes that came from my trip was the custard bun 流沙包 – which literally translates as 'leaking sandy bun'. It's a classic dim sum, made up of steamed fluffy wheat flour dough wrapped around a salted egg yolk custard. Traditionally, the recipe uses loads of salted egg yolk inside to get the sandy texture required. There are no sauces in European gastronomy that pride themselves on achieving a 'sandy texture'. Young chefs get hot pans thrown at them if their sauces are not all silky smooth and lump free, and the idea of a salty custard definitely isn't something familiar to a European palate. Custard, though, holds very strong nostalgic memories for any Brit above the age of thirty. As children, it was fed to us on a daily basis for school lunches, usually served by a large, intimidating lady who would slap it into your bowl as you walked down the queue. Having grown up in this world, custard instantly grabbed my attention. I had to make it fire out of the bun and ooze as dramatically as possible, so I adjusted the recipe and the look. And now, that custard bun has attained a social media life of its own. What my exploding, not-so-salty custard bun has shown me is the potential to remodel people's preconceptions of one of the world's most loved cuisines, to make the unfamiliar familiar and the familiar curiously unfamiliar. A restaurant opened in London recently called Egg Slut, in honour of the oozing, exploding quality of a yolk and its invaluable 'insta' attraction. Interestingly, though, in China, the custard bun simply doesn't have the same kudos.

It's now been seventeen years since I started cooking – seventeen years of jotting notes and doodles in notebooks of dishes that I enjoyed in various places across China, recipes that I stole from other chefs to use in the restaurant. But then I met Dr Mukta Das, the food anthropologist and research associate at the SOAS Food Studies Centre. Our relationship is very special, mainly because her passion for history meets my desire to push myself, her ability to converse simply and broadly meets my chef-like attention span. What started out with her supplying me with historical poetry, photos of historical vessels and tableware – to give me a sense of how the handful of recipes that survive to this day can be imagined – has now become us hanging out *Sopranos*-style with conversations outdoors and sipping on espressos.

The work that I do with Mukta at my restaurant A. Wong today marks the first time that I have no longer 'copied' contemporary chefs. It's the first time that we have begun to carve out our own path, one that is about taking the best from the past, not plagiarising the present. Our conversations dig into China's convoluted past, using it to create dishes that I hope could one day become the 'traditions and authenticity' of the future. The journey is about me negotiating the predicament of being British born, with a European culinary education, being a British-Chinese chef and a Chinese restaurateur in an international city, and using food research to navigate these parts of who I am in developing new dishes.

In my opinion, the skill and refinement of technique that exists within the 3,000-year-old Chinese kitchen is un-paralleled with any other cuisine of the world. The first official Chinese restaurant landed in the US in 1849, and in the UK around 1908, yet, over 100 years later, the perception of this cuisine is still deemed inferior to other cuisines. It's still the food that you go to when you've drunk too much to care about your tastebuds. Why is this?

But actually the more that I work with Mukta and the more that I cook, the more I realise that the taste of food is chemical and cultural. Cultural relevance and cultural importance play a role in the eating experience. Culture, flavour, texture – they all go hand in hand. If what I did was strictly about cooking, I certainly would never have become a chef. This isn't just a transaction of turning raw produce into cooked produce to make money. I enjoy the idea of facilitating the affinity of sitting around a table, being a spectator to the unmeasurable magic that happens through these interactions and the social implications that these can have on both individuals and wider cultures.

A few months back, I was having a philosophical discussion with my four-year-old son Ayden. I got the impression my son was taught that everyone in the world was the same but I realised I wanted my kids to know that they were different, that they came from an ethnic background with its own beauties, probably because I grew up with my parents constantly reminding me that 'I wasn't British'. So what? Well the problem with not feeling British when you are British Born Chinese is that you are effectively left being 'nothing' because mainlanders don't think of you as being Chinese either. In working with Mukta though, I have almost managed to find comfort and peace in being seen as neither truly British nor Chinese through the empowerment of knowledge, but instead I have found my own vantage point and understand my own prejudices, through the lens of food.

The London and global restaurant scene is constantly changing and there's a lot of foreign investment flying around. People assume that you can pick up a restaurant in China that has three Michelin stars and just plonk it into London, Paris or New York expecting it to flourish as it does in China, to expect the veil of apparent 'motherland authenticity' to ensure success. It never works that way, these restaurants nearly always fail. My work with Mukta tries to bridge this gap. I want to be able to relate and empathise with both Chinese and international guests who have very idiosyncratic expectations of Chinese food. By understanding our guests' past and their relationship with the cuisine from a multi-sociological perspective, yet using my understanding of British cultural nuances, we attempt to implant culturally specific, subconscious nostalgia into dishes – making dishes relatable – where the unfamiliar can become the familiar and the familiar can turn into the curiously unfamiliar in building excitement and affinity around a dinner table.

Heritage (The Stories We Tell)

Tuyen Do

When I was first asked to write a piece that reflected my heritage, I said yes without thinking, I had such a visceral reaction to the word. Even now, as I'm writing, I feel it in my body, my bones, and surprising tears form in the corners of my eyes. How can one word have such power? As I attempt to formulate these feelings, I find that they are a muddle of conflicting messages and information that defies efforts to be arranged into neatly constructed arguments. They range from pride in one's own cultural background to seeing it used as a weapon; from the feeling of home and connectiveness, to a sense of alienation and distinct lack of belonging. 'Heritage' is a word that conjures up euphoric feelings of love and celebration, yet at the same time a primal fear of being separate. How do I illustrate this in an essay? Is this something that I need to solve? Is it something that can be explained? Because what does Heritage mean? Like many other words of this kind – 'identity' being another – it is as personal as the shape of our noses or the shade, tone and texture of our skin. So, I am going to do what I know how to do: tell you my story.

I am the youngest of seven children and a Vietnamese refugee. When I was a little girl, there would be a taint of embarrassment whenever this word was uttered. An imperceptible draw back, or a slight lowering of the eyes. My family, like many exiled Vietnamese, arrived in England with nothing but '*hai bàn tay trắng*'- two empty palms. We relied on the kindness and charity of others. It was something my parents were extremely grateful for, but, at the same time, would have to endure, swallowing the daily micro-humiliations that came with it. As a child I absorbed this without having the words to describe it. Now, as a woman beginning her forties, I am still trying to find the right ones. The best I can do in an effort to communicate this feeling is to compare it to that constant low-level anxiety you feel when you're in someone else's impeccable house, fearing you might spill your brown tea on their beautiful white rug. Don't mess up, don't make a fuss, and be thankful you've been invited.

> I was once a refugee, although no one would mistake me for being a refugee now. Because of this, I insist on being called a refugee, since the temptation to pretend that I am not a refugee is strong.
>
> – Viet Thanh Nguyen, *The Displaced*

I remember very clearly, aged fourteen, a package arriving at our house. It was a big event. There was something in this thick A4 envelope that engendered respect and a sense that something historic was about to occur. We gathered in the lounge as a family to witness 'the opening'. My mother knelt behind my father in the middle of the room, her hands resting gently on his shoulders. The rest of us sat on the floor surrounding them. I looked on dispassionately, a little irritated at being called from whatever I was into at that age (probably listening to the Cranberries and wishing I had the same ethereal abandon). All eyes were on my father, whose hands were shaking ever so slightly as he carefully, almost surgically, peeled open the seam. *It is this moment that has seared itself into my memory.* My father, who to this point had never once shown any emotion, shed tears. They streamed down his face and didn't stop. It felt like a deep well had finally overflowed. He looked up to the sky and said, 'Thank you, God. Thank you, God,' doing the sign of the cross. Finally he pulled out what we were all waiting for, the mystery contents. Small burgundy booklets with flashes of gold. Was this a miracle? Maybe it was? It felt like one. On closer inspection, the gold that emblazoned the front of these magical packets was the coat of arms of the United Kingdom. In his hands were our first passports. One for each member of the family. This was a historic moment. The passports were handed out excitedly like tickets to a concert. I remember staring at mine, and individually stroking the colourful pages. When I got to the end, there I was, my fourteen-year-old self staring out at me. And next to that, under Nationality, were two words that changed our lives forever. We were no longer refugees, but citizens. I was now a British citizen. From then on, I sank further into this new label I had already started to cultivate. I was British.

Aged seventeen, I am forced to go on an organised trip to France with the Vietnamese Catholic community for World Youth Day, which took place in Paris that year. The main aim was to be blessed by Pope John Paul II, along with over a million others. We rode a minibus all the way to a campsite just outside the city, with no stops. It was an uncomfortable journey devoid of any luxury, the sole aim being to get from A to B. It was dark when we arrived and were taken to our sleeping quarters, which consisted of rickety camp beds, metal frames covered by a tarpaulin, lined neatly in large tents. I thought of my warm duvet back in London and marvelled at how all these Vietnamese people seemed instantly at home with such a set-up; walking around in flip flops, smiling, toothbrushes sticking out of their mouths, coming out of the shared bathrooms and saying hello to one another as if we were old friends. In the morning, we had our orientation and met with other Vietnamese Catholics from all over Europe. It was the first time I had come into contact with others like myself in such large numbers. Not the Catholic part, but young, Vietnamese, and speaking another language. Except they didn't speak English, but spoke Dutch, French, German and more. They all looked amazing, sounded amazing, and seemed so cool, like anyone from the continent seems to be, whether you're brown, Black or white. I was instantly captivated. I wanted to be with them, be part of them, even to go as far as rub myself against them (but that's another story). The grumpiness I had woken up with after a cold, uncomfortable, sleepless night disappeared. It was exciting to be at this campsite, where we were all connected by something strong but intangible. More than just the shared language, which was not English, but Vietnamese. More than just the colour of our skin. But our unsaid, unarticulated experiences.

In the beginning, I felt tongue-tied and embarrassed that my language skills had disintegrated so badly. But the excitement and feeling like being a lost penguin finding other penguins in a sea of seals forced me to persevere. After a few days, speaking Vietnamese became as natural to me as coming from my mother's womb. I felt a freedom I had never felt before. A freedom from questions about who I was, where I was from, what I was; just for that brief amount of time, and it was great. Riding on this high, when I was asked to do a reading in Vietnamese for mass that week, I agreed, feeling emboldened by my experience. Afterwards, two older Vietnamese men came to speak to me. They asked me where I was from. I said London. They asked me how old I was. I said seventeen. They asked me how old I was when I left Vietnam. I said four. Then they said, what a pity. What a pity for you. A Vietnamese girl who can't speak Vietnamese. You must feel so ashamed. *It is this moment that has seared itself into my memory.* I did feel shame, so much of it that I could no longer look at them. I could no longer stand there; I didn't have the strength. I didn't have the tools to combat their belittling stares, to argue my point, to know what point I should be making, to say that even though my pronunciation wasn't clear, I could understand everything they were saying to me, and it wasn't my fault that they couldn't hear me. But instead, all I could do was run away, back to the tarpaulin camp bed, and heave salty tears. The sorrow was immense.

Aged twenty-three, I am in the restaurant kitchen with my mum. I am a restaurateur. After sleeping through the university experience, I had tried and failed to fit into the 'Accountant' box, and somehow found my way back to hospitality. It was a world I knew well growing up. A world I vowed I would never come back to, but life has a way of making you face the things you try to run away from. There wasn't a choice. I had been rejected from any decent graduate programme out there due to my introversion. It was a prerequisite that you needed to be able to speak up and be heard. Something I was still struggling with. We were in the kitchen preparing the sauces for that evening's service. Both my mother and I had spent hours tinkering about with the recipes in order to create the best result: returning customers. For her this meant success, and success meant money, and money meant safety. For me, it was my way of becoming financially independent, and hopefully moving out of home and away from my mother's grasp.

By now I was very proficient at whizzing around the kitchen and whipping up our secrets. My mother, being the person she was, trusted no one with the recipes so it fell on my shoulders to make them all. She would then go round with a chopstick, dip it in the sauce, taste and give her assessment. This one needed more sugar, this one more salt, the lemons this week are not as astringent so more juice, don't overdo it on the fish sauce or no one will come back. At the famous 'Vietnamese dipping sauce', that now regularly makes it into the *The Times'* magazine on Saturdays in various guises, she stops to pay particular attention. She relays one of her well-told stories about the first time she saw a customer lick the 'Bún Xạ'' lemongrass noodles bowl clean. He ate it with such heartiness and gusto that not only did he not leave a trace of food, he also proceeded to pick up the remaining sauce and drink it like lemonade, smacking his lips in satisfaction. She laughed big full-bellied laughs as she talked, shaking her head in disbelief at the appetite of big burly white men. It was absurd to drink fish sauce, but this, she reminded me, was the effect we were going for. I did not mind. It was part of our routine.

After the dinner rush was over, my mother and father would sit at their regular table and ask me to make them their favourite 'Cảnh Chua Cá Thià Là', hot and sour fish soup with dill. This is also my favourite dish. Harmonising the sweet and the sour is the art of Vietnamese cooking. I fry the ginger, garlic and chilli until they release their aromas and start to brown, then I add tomatoes and stock. I season with tamarind, sugar, salt and fish sauce to a fine balance, add the fried fish and let it simmer. Finally, I reach for the magic ingredient that my mother taught me: beer. It froths and bubbles satisfyingly and then settles to a mellow hum. When it is done, I add a generous helping of dill and finely sliced spring onions, ladle the food into a large bowl, dish up an equally large bowl of rice and carry it up to my waiting parents. We sit. My dad mumbles the Lord's Prayer, and then I wait for the verdict. 'My God!' my mother would say. 'This girl can really cook. It's delicious, old man. Eat! My daughter has the gift. The gift of a good tongue.' *These moments are also seared into my memory.* Seeing my father suck the flavour from his favourite part of the fish, its head, a smile spreads from my heart to my face, and I eat with them.

Fast forward nearly twenty years to today, and a lot has changed, both for me and the environment in which we live. The two inextricably interlinked. I have long moved on from the restaurant and have undergone a kind of rebirth. I found a love of drama, and through drama I proceeded to go on a road of discovery, seeing myself from the outside in as well as the inside out. As an actor, I have been able to experience myself in many different guises that are not my own, but also in a way that I deeply understand through our universal human experience. I have come to shape and create stories of my own in order to process my past and connect to my future. I have seen that work move and affect others, and I have met with people across the globe who are doing similar things. I have, in effect, woken up from my slumber, from being trapped in my own skin, and have learnt to celebrate who I am, and to see myself in others. But on the flip-side,

I have also been made more aware than ever of the prejudice, discrimination and injustices that come with being judged wholly on the shape of my nose and the shade, tone and texture of my skin.

When we think of heritage, we usually think of the past, and the things that are passed down to us. Culture, language, food. Throughout my years, I have been asked the question 'Where are you from?' many, many, many times. Even writing it down now makes me sigh with tiredness. I try to answer it with good humour, as it is usually asked from a place of sincere curiosity. In recent years, the conversation about race and representation has changed to the extent that you can no longer ignore the layers of underlying ignorance that accompany it. So, the question has altered slightly to 'What is your heritage?', which amounts to the same thing. These three memories have come from the hazy images of my past, but they are also my attempt at answering that question because, to be honest, I don't know the answer. The short answer would be to say, 'I was born in Vietnam; yes, I can speak Vietnamese; and yes, the food is amazing', but the truth is far more complex and interesting. And maybe that's why I said yes to writing this piece. Because I wanted the opportunity to leave an imprint of what my heritage might be. Not just for me, but for others who may read these pages and see themselves reflected. For future generations and for my son, who could one day pick up this book.

Our heritage is our story. The stories we listen to, the things we see, the people we grew up with, the journeys we've travelled. We understand the heritage of others to be derived from the same things. The stories we hear about them, the things we see about them, the people we see them with, and the journeys they share with us. Through this lens, we can shape our heritage to be what we want it to be. A sharing of knowledge and experiences to connect us as human beings, or a way to divide and alienate us from each other. My greatest hope is that we do the former and unpick the latter. We celebrate and share in our differences – differences that also echo our similarities, and acknowledge and denounce narratives that do the opposite. I am here to tell you my story, and this is me.

This is me

So they told me
write from what you know
from deep within your heart
then they told me
write about anything
about anyone
about anywhere
then they told me
wow you're interesting
that voice

it's new, it's unique

it's a first

stick to that

then they told me

oh no

not another family

people from somewhere else

being here

being other

oh no

not again

so I told them

this is me

my unique voice

this is love

this is loss

beginnings and endings

struggle and triumph

tenderness and hurt

then they told me

no

you should write about anyone

from anywhere

dealing with anything

you should be able

you should be able

you should be able

you're more than this

then they told me
oh no
not another couple
about people from somewhere else
being here being other
but that voice
it's new, it's unique
it's interesting
stick to that
so I told them
this is me
my unique voice
my love
my loss
my darkness and my light
my violence and my healing touch
then they told me
no
we want that other story
from your other place
the place you came from
not here
being other
but the other
being there
the other struggle
the other hurt
the other violence

the new, new unique voice
so then I screamed
and I railed
and I scratched out my eyes
and pulled at my face
and turned out my skin
and clawed at the beating of my heart
until there was quiet

until there was nothing

until there was death
in silence

but in the darkness came
tiny whispers
they came to me in a dream
from the past
and the future
and everything in between

this is you
this is you
this is you

and this is your place
this is your other
from somewhere else
and here
descended from somewhere else

and here
carved deep in the lines
of your face
and your hands
and your eyes
and the deep crevices beside your mouth
this is you
this is you
this is you
the infinite place
of love
and loss
and envy
and hate
and rage
and dirt
and loathing
of life
and death
and hope
and light
and kindness
and growth
and healing

this is you
this is you
this is you

this is me
this is me
this is me

this is me.

My name is Tuyen Do. I am an actor and writer of mixed Vietnamese and Chinese descent, born in Vietnam, raised in the UK. And this is my heritage.

Contributors

Amy Poon

Amy Poon was born in London and educated at Keble College, University of Oxford, where she obtained a third class degree in Japanese, and has lived in Geneva, Tokyo, Sydney and Singapore. A jack of all trades and master of none, she has tutored in French and Latin, worked as a hostess, marketed Patek Philippe watches, opened a champagne bar in Singapore's red-light district, sold contemporary Asian art, run an event company, sat on the board of the UN Women, Singapore and written two books. She returned to London in 2018 to resurrect the family food business that she vowed never to get involved in.

Amy recommends: 'Shanghai Tang' by Francis Yip – the theme tune of the classic Chinese TV series, *The Bund*, rivals *The Godfather* for intrigue and drama, style and glamour, love and loss. It makes my heart stir every time I hear it! Also, for obvious reasons, the film *Eat Drink Man Woman* by Ang Lee.

Andrew Wong

Andrew Wong is a chef, anthropologist and cultural observer. He is British born, of Chinese heritage – his environment and nurture have had an equal impact. Combined with a strong academic background, the marriage of both has led to a cooking style that has one foot placed firmly in the future and the other inspired by the past. Andrew opened A.Wong in 2012 with his wife Nathalie – the A paying homage to his parents Albert and Annie. In 2017 A.Wong was awarded its first Michelin star, and a second followed in 2021. Andrew also collaborates with food anthropologist Dr Mukta Das for their podcast *XO Soused*; season two is available now.

Andrew recommends: Zhang Daqian, a Chinese artist who painted using traditional techniques whilst exploring contemporary ideas and movements. I love the spontaneity and colours in his splashed ink landscape paintings.

Anna Sulan Masing

Anna Sulan Masing is a writer, academic and poet based in London. Her PhD looked at how identity changes when space and location change. She is the co-founder of *Cheese* magazine and *Sourced*, a publication that looks at food systems. She launched her podcast series, *A Taste of Place* by Whetstone Radio Collective, in 2022. Her debut book, *Chinese and Other Asian*, will be published in February 2024.

Anna recommends: reading, looking and experiencing the work of the London-based artist Youngsook Choi, who is a feminist geographer and also explores ideas of nature.

Catherine Cho

Catherine Cho is a literary agent and author of *Inferno: A Memoir of Motherhood and Madness,* which was shortlisted for the *Sunday Times* Young Writer Award and the Jhalak Prize. She founded her own agency, Paper Literary, in 2020. Originally from the US, she lives in London with her family.

Catherine recommends: The debut short story collection *A Thousand Years of Good Prayers* by Yiyun Li. It's the first of an astonishing series of work. Yiyun Li came to the US from Beijing as an immunologist, and she started writing as an adult. She has been described as writing the stories of her homeland in the language of the nation she emigrated to. The precision of her language, the depth of the characterisations is haunting. There is a loneliness in her work that feels universal, I find that I have to be prepared when I read her stories because the truth of it can be shattering.

Claire Kohda

Claire Kohda is an author and violinist from Margate. Her literary debut novel, *Woman, Eating,* is about a Japanese-Malaysian-English vampire dealing with all sorts of hunger – hunger for a sense of cultural identity and belonging, for friendship, love and blood. It is published by Virago (UK) and Harper Collins (US). The novel has been optioned for TV, with Claire adapting. Claire is also a book critic and has written on art; her reviews and essays have appeared in the *Guardian*, the *TLS*, the *New York Times*, *Harper's Bazaar* and elsewhere. As a violinist, she's played with Sigur Rós, The National, Anna Meredith and Jessie Ware, and on film soundtracks including *The Matrix Resurrections* and *The Two Popes*.

Claire recommends: Where The Wild Ladies Are by Matsuda Aoko (published by Tilted Axis Press, translated by Polly Barton), which retells traditional Japanese ghost stories through a feminist lens. Stories in which women are turned into monsters by their rage and jealousy are transformed so that that rage and jealousy are characters' sources of power. In one story, a woman embraces her body hair after she is dumped and is changed into a monster completely covered in hair; she proclaims, 'I [am] an amazing thing!' This book celebrates what is considered repulsive in women by traditional standards. I just love that it exists.

Gemma Chan

The actress and producer Gemma Chan is well known for her roles in the BAFTA-nominated artificial intelligence drama *Humans*; the film adaptation of Kevin Kwan's best-selling novel, *Crazy Rich Asians*; and Marvel Studios' *Captain Marvel*. In 2020, Gemma starred opposite Meryl Streep in Steven Soderbergh's comedy *Let Them All Talk*, and in 2021, she voiced Namaari in Disney's *Raya and the Last Dragon*. She also led an ensemble cast in *Eternals*, directed by Chloé Zhao. Gemma will soon be seen in Apple's *Extrapolations*, an anthology series about climate change helmed by Scott Z. Burns, and in Olivia Wilde's psychological thriller, *Don't Worry Darling*. Alongside Working Title Films and producer Nina Yang Bongiovi, Gemma is developing a feature film, in which she will star, about legendary Hollywood actress Anna May Wong, considered to be the best-known Chinese-American actress during Hollywood's golden age. Gemma will also star in a spinoff of *Crazy Rich Asians* which will centre around her character.

Gemma is also an accomplished theatre actress, performing in *Yellow Face* by the Tony Award winning David Henry Hwang and in Harold Pinter's *The Homecoming* at Trafalgar Studios. Gemma is a Unicef UK Ambassador and has helped launch a GoFundMe initiative, which provides grants to grassroots organisations supporting East and South East Asian (ESEA) and broader communities in the UK (Gofundme.com/esea).

Gemma recommends: *Minor Feelings* by Cathy Park Hong and *Interior Chinatown* by Charles Yu.

Helena Lee

Helena Lee is the features director of *Harper's Bazaar*, and is responsible for all the art and culture content. She also co-edits the annual magazine *Bazaar Art* that celebrates women in the art world and launched *Bazaar Art Week* in 2018, which was shortlisted for the BSME Best Innovation Award. In February 2020, she founded the platform East Side Voices to raise the visibility of East and Southeast Asian talent. She is a Platform Presents Playwright judge, a founding member of the Ginsburg Health Board and a visiting lecturer at City University.

Helena recommends: Dear Girls by the US comedian Ali Wong. It was a sad day when I realised that the pandemic also meant Ali Wong's UK tour was cancelled, so every now and then I read this book – part memoir, part manifesto – just to remind myself of what I'm missing and can snort with laughter at all the Asian things that I did, and didn't realise. I also enjoy the pithy, off-beat writing of the actor and dramatist Vera Chok. She is one to watch.

June Bellebono

June Bellebono is a cultural producer, writer, educator and model. June founded and runs *oestrogeneration*, an online magazine platform highlighting transfeminine voices in the UK, and founded and hosts Queer Good Grief, a peer support group created by and for bereaved LGBTQ+ people. June has produced events for Decolonise Fest, Autograph ABP, We Exist, Museum of the Home, London College of Fashion and Free Word. June's writing can be found online at *gal-dem*, *daikon**, *Remember and Resist*, *PEN Transmissions* and *i News*. June has been featured in many DIY zines and she's one of the writers in the anthology *Letters from the Grief Club: How we Live with Loss* (2022). When not working, they can be found dancing and serving looks in grotty basements and night clubs until the early hours of the morning all around London.

June recommends: As I mention in my piece, *Smile As They Bow* by Nu Nu Yi was a lifechanging book for me. I also wanted to give a shout out to the Burmese music collective Bouhinga.

Katie Leung

A Scottish born and bred Chinese actor working part time to fund her love of Guinness and pay rent. Graduated with a BA (Hons) degree in Fine Art Photography, dropped out of finance school and then graduated with a BA degree in

Acting. Favourite job: *The World of Extreme Happiness,* written by Frances Ya Chu Cowhig for The Shed at the National Theatre in London. Food favourites: Siu Mai, Zhong Zi, mum's soup and beef brisket with rice/noodles. Eldest of five. Feminist. She/Her.

Katie recommends: Kae Alexander. Actor/Writer　我最親愛的大家姐

Mary Jean Chan

Mary Jean Chan is the author of *Flèche*, published by Faber & Faber (2019) and Faber USA (2020). *Flèche* won the 2019 Costa Book Award for Poetry and was selected as a Poetry Book Society Recommendation. *Flèche* has also been short-listed for the International Dylan Thomas Prize, the John Pollard Foundation International Poetry Prize, the Jhalak Prize, the Seamus Heaney Centre First Collection Poetry Prize and a Lambda Literary Award. In 2018, Chan won the Poetry Society Geoffrey Dearmer Prize. They were shortlisted for the Forward Prizes in the Best Single Poem category in 2017 and 2019, receiving an Eric Gregory Award in 2019. Chan served as guest co-editor alongside Will Harris at *The Poetry Review* (Spring 2020) and recently co-edited *100 Queer Poems* (Vintage, 2022) with Andrew McMillan. In 2022, they will be a writer-in-residence at the Nanyang Technological University School of Humanities in Singapore. Born and raised in Hong Kong, Chan is

Senior Lecturer in Creative Writing (Poetry) at Oxford Brookes University and serves as a supervisor on the MSt in Creative Writing at the University of Oxford.

Mary Jean recommends: 'Poplar Street' by the Chinese-American poet Chen Chen, because it's a gorgeous poem that speaks to our universal desire for meaningful connection with others, and how prejudice can jeopardise even the strongest of familial relationships.

Naomi Shimada

Born in Tokyo to a Japanese father and a Dutch/British mother, she feels as though she truly is a child of two worlds. Through her modelling, podcasting, radio and book writing work, she imagines a more viable and just future that tries to bring her many worlds together. She has spent the last 15 years in the modelling industry advocating for widening the lens on what and how we think of beauty. She spends her life learning and being inquisitive about the things that bring people together. Shimada co-authored *Mixed Feelings*, a book that explores the emotional impact of our digital habits and takes a closer look at what happens to us when we use our apps. Her podcast on the BBC, *Beauty Fix*, is a curious dip into the world of beauty where she speaks to people about their perspectives on the world and seeks to understand what beauty means to them.

Naomi recommends: Sunshowers 1989, by Nami Shimada – a Japanese house DJ/producer – is an ode to the dance floor. I was such a club kid growing up, the dance floor was where I found myself and I just love the thought of this breaking so many cross cultural boundaries, it was a huge hit at the Paradise garage and was played by all the big club heads at the time. It's so timeless and makes me proud to be almost name twins!

Romalyn Ante

Romalyn Ante is a Filipino-British poet, author and specialist nurse practitioner. She is the co-founding editor of *harana poetry* and *Tsaá with Roma*. She is the first East Asian to win the international Poetry London Prize as well as the Manchester Poetry Prize. Her work has been featured in BBC World News, BBC Radio 4, *Harper's Bazaar*, *Vogue UK*, *World Literature Today*, amongst others. Her debut poetry collection is *Antiemetic for Homesickness* (Chatto & Windus). She was recently awarded the Jerwood Compton Fellowship.

Romalyn recommends: 'Middle Name with Diacritics', a poem by Natalie Linh Bolderston. This poem is a tapestry of striking images that explore familial and historical pain and narratives of survival.

Rowan Hisayo Buchanan

Rowan Hisayo Buchanan is the author of *Harmless Like You* and *Starling Days*. She has won the Authors' Club Best First Novel Award and a Betty Trask Award and been shortlisted for the Costa Novel Award. Her work has been a *New York Times* Editors' Choice, an *NPR* Great Read, and recommended by *O, the Oprah Magazine*. Her short work has appeared in several places including *Granta Guernica*, and the *Harvard Review*. She is the editor of the *Go Home!* anthology.

Rowan recommends: Yoko Ogawa's *The Memory Police* and Sharlene Teo's *Ponti*. (The latter is not just because I love her as a human – it genuinely is one of my favourite books.)

Sharlene Teo

Sharlene Teo's debut novel *Ponti* won the Deborah Rogers Foundation Writers Award, was shortlisted for the Hearst Big Book Award and Edward Stanford Fiction Award and longlisted for the Jhalak Prize. Her work has been translated into eleven languages and published in places such as the *TLS*, *McSweeney's*, LitHub, the *Guardian* and the Daunt Books anthology *At the Pond*.

Sharlene recommends: *The Wandering* by Intan Paramaditha – a choose your own adventure novel about global nomadism, by one of the most original and brilliantly Gothic visionaries in fiction today.

Tash Aw

Tash Aw was born in Taipei to Malaysian parents. He grew up in Kuala Lumpur and moved to Britain to attend university. He is the author of four critically-acclaimed novels, including, most recently, *We, the Survivors*, as well as a family memoir, *Strangers on a Pier*. His work has been translated into twenty-three languages.

Tash recommends: I Don't Want to Sleep Alone by Tsai Ming-liang, a haunting interrogation of loneliness and rootlessness, set against a backdrop of a Kuala Lumpur that feels both derelict and utterly contemporary – the most evocative portrait of the city in modern cinema.

Tuyen Do

Tuyen Do is an actor and writer. She has worked extensively on stage and screen. Places of work include the National Theatre, Royal Court Theatre, Hampstead Theatre, Bunker Theatre, BBC, Legendary Pictures and more. Her writing has been performed at the Park Theatre, Bristol Old Vic, Arcola, Theatre 503, and Ovalhouse Theatre. Published credits include *Summer Rolls*, and a contribution to *Hear Me Now: Audition Monologues for Actors of Colour*. In 2019 she founded VanThanh Productions with Tuyet Van Huynh as a way to promote and nurture stories from minority backgrounds.

Tuyen recommends: The play *Vietgone* by Vietnamese American writer Qui Nguyen. This is a refugee love story that subverts and explodes all of your ideas of what that might be. It is brilliantly funny, sexy, original, and has emotional resonance for anyone who has ever struggled and been in love. The characters are big, and full, and you will not want it to stop. I adore this play, and I am sure you will too.

Will Harris

Will Harris is a writer of Chinese Indonesian and British heritage, born and based in London. His debut poetry book, *RENDANG*, was a Poetry Book Society Choice and won the Forward Prize for Best First Collection. His second collection, *Brother Poem*, will be published in 2023.

Will recommends: DMZ Colony by Don Mee Choi, a book about South Korea and the United States composed of poetry, prose, drawings and photographs, which is also an essay in the broadest sense, brushing history against the grain of experience, with translation a necessary tool of anti-neocolonial resistance.

Zing Tsjeng

Zing Tsjeng is an author, journalist and presenter based in London. She is currently the editor in chief of VICE UK and the host of its video series *Empires of Dirt* and the BBC Sounds podcast *United Zingdom*. Her four-book series *Forgotten Women* was published by Octopus in 2018 and her writing has been highly commended at the British Journalism Awards. She was appointed Visiting Professor of Creative Media at Oxford University in 2021.

Zing recommends: America is not the Heart by Elaine Castillo is one of my favourite books of the last few years. I knew very little about the Filipino-American experience before picking up the novel, and was absolutely blown away by its enormous depth and empathy. I was absolutely bereft that I had to leave the characters behind when I finished the novel.